GOOD EATING

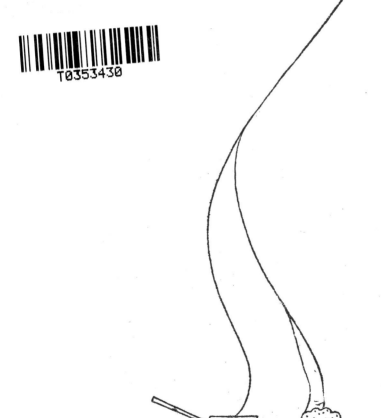

GOOD EATING

A SECOND BOOK OF
WAR-TIME RECIPES

compiled by

The Daily Telegraph
HOME COOK

This edition published 2014 by Pan Books
an imprint of Pan Macmillan, a division of Macmillan Publishers Limited
Pan Macmillan, 20 New Wharf Road, London N1 9RR
Basingstoke and Oxford
Associated companies throughout the world
www.panmacmillan.com

978-1-4472-7381-3

The Macmillan Group has no responsibility for the information
provided by and author websites whose address you obtain from
this book ('author websites'). The inclusion of author website
addresses in this book does not constitute an endorsement by or
association with us of such sites or the content, products,
advertising or other materials presented on such sites.

A CIP catalogue record for this book is available from
the British Library.

Visit **www.panmacmillan.com** to read more about all our books and to buy
them. You will also find features, author interviews and news of any author
events, and you can sign up for e-newsletters so that you're always first to hear
about our new releases.

Contents

(continued overleaf)

Contents *(cont.)*

SECTION III

Snack Service

SECTION IV

Stocking the Store Cupboard

SECTION V

Art of Flavouring

Foreword

COOKERY, always influenced by wars and social changes, has come to one of its greatest turning points. Time saving not only for the few but for all women is now of vital consideration.

Much that belongs to the old cookery books has become unsuited to modern housekeeping. It is to the home cooks rather than to the food specialists and the scientists that we must now look for the most practical and pleasing solutions of new problems. Day by day they are conducting quietly in their own kitchens painstaking, purposeful research producing the attractive fare that will constitute the basis of post-war cookery. In this way they are mastering a new technique.

Special sections deal with Snack Service; All-the-year-round Store Cupboard Stocking; Home Kitchen Lead with *Daily Telegraph* tested prize recipes; Art of Flavouring. The purpose of this book is to provide tested recipes for general use in meeting the requirements of Today and Tomorrow.

The Daily Telegraph HOME COOK.

OVEN CHART			
Oven heat	Gas		Electricity (Thermometer figure)
	Number control	Letter control	
			° F.
Very hot . . .	8 or 9	G	500
Hot . . .	7	F	450
Fairly hot. . .	6	E–F	400
Moderate . .	5	E	375
Very moderate . .	3 or 4	D	350
Cool . . .	2	C	300
Slow . . .	½–1	B	275
Very slow. . .	¼–½	A	250

NOTE. Control numbers and letters for gas oven are those of a large number of ovens and should be regarded as an approximate guide.

SECTION 1

WARTIME HOUSEKEEPING

Chapter I: MAIN DISH COOKERY

HOME catering nowadays centres round the main dish instead of the creation of the meal of many courses.

The joint has survived years of rationing; it suits our national habits and tastes too well to be discarded. It has however had to change radically. The small joints now familiar are the one-time "stewing meats"—the cheaper cuts which are profitable from the ration point of view. Some of them were unknown a few years ago to numbers of housewives who are surprised at their excellence. Such meats usually need to be rolled and stuffed to make a sizeable joint with which the carver can deal. Forcemeat therefore is important in meat cookery.

These new joints may be roasted, boiled, braised or pot-roasted—a fuel-saving method this last which adds to flavour. Marinading is practised by housewives for a joint that is likely to be tough or flavourless. This method also preserves meat that is not to be cooked immediately.

(a) THE JOINTS of TODAY

Cheaper cuts popularised by the ration in place of the old-time joints and sure of favour in post-war cookery include:

Beef: brisket, flank, leg, skirt.

Mutton: breast, best, middle and scrag end of neck.

Veal: breast, knuckle, neck.

9

BEEF SKIRT ROAST

Skirt of beef.	2 tomatoes.
Herb stuffing (*see* force-	
meat for flank).	

This cut is tender, full of flavour and makes a rich gravy. Is excellent roasted or in a meat pudding or pie.

Ask butcher to cut in one piece skirt of beef, stuff with savoury forcemeat, add if liked sliced tomatoes before rolling up. Tie each end and centre. Roast, basting well. Serve with roast potatoes, other vegetable and thick gravy.—MRS. L. BRISTOW, 43 Manor Drive, Hinchley Wood, Esher.

BOILED BEEF AND DUMPLINGS

2 lbs. salt silverside of beef.	1 parsnip (optional).
	A few peppercorns.
2 onions.	Small cabbage.
3 carrots.	Sprigs of thyme and pars-
2 turnips.	ley or dried herbs.

Wash meat. If very salt, soak a few hours in cold water. Put joint into saucepan of cold water to cover, bring to boil. Simmer 1 hour.

Peel and cut up vegetables, the carrots lengthwise, and add with peppercorns and herbs to meat. Cover and simmer 15 minutes. Then add dumplings and simmer for another 20 minutes.

To make Dumplings

3 ozs. flour.	1½ ozs. suet or cooking
Pinch of salt.	fat.
	Water to mix.

Mix to a dough with cold water. Form into small balls.

BREAST OF MUTTON OR LAMB

2 breasts of mutton or lamb.	Mint and parsley.
	Seasoning.
1 handful oatmeal.	Water.
Spring onions or chives.	

With sharp pointed knife remove bones from meat, also centre layer of fat from pointed end. Flatten meat. Mix oatmeal with chopped onion, herbs, seasoning and a little water. Spread on meat, roll tightly and tie or sew up end to make joint neat.

Place bones in bottom of meat tin with a little seasoned water, put meat on bones, lightly dredge with flour, put fat that has been removed on top. Bake in very hot oven, lower temperature after 15 minutes, cook 1 hour. Excellent hot or cold.—E. M. G., Bruton House, Mortimer West, Nr. Reading.

BRISKET ROAST

"Too fat, they won't eat it" is the housewife's comment when the butcher offers brisket—regretful, for round about 2s. provides presentable family joint. Follow this method of roasting.

Put joint in dripping tin containing sufficient water to cover bottom. Place on top of meat any bits of fat, oddments of lard or margarine. After 15 minutes at full roasting heat, cover joint and continue to cook slowly.

Eat cold, when fat will be found to be very mellow, and meat, thinly sliced, extremely tender. A good basinful of dripping is yielded.

Another way of dealing with brisket is to put joint in saucepan with water just to cover, a few cloves, peppercorns, and if available a bayleaf and a sprig of thyme. Bring to boiling point, simmer till tender in tightly covered pan.—*The Daily Telegraph* HOME COOK.

NECK OF MUTTON OR LAMB

Best end neck of mutton   Mint or onion stuffing.
    or lamb.

Having boned meat and stuffed it, roll it up, tie round centre and across ends. Roast it with any pieces of surplus fat on top, baste well. Bake potatoes round joint. Use bones to make soup.

PORK POT ROAST

2 lbs. lean pork.   *For Apple Sauce:*
1 cabbage.   ½ lb. apples.
2 carrots.   Nutmeg.
1 turnip.   ¼ gill water.
2 shallots or onion.   1 teaspoonful sugar.
Sage; seasoning.
1 pint stock or water.

Pot-roasting saves fuel. Trim piece of fat from joint, place in saucepan, when very hot put in meat and brown both sides. Remove joint.

Shred cabbage, slice carrots, turnip, onion, put in pan, season. Place joint on top, sprinkle with flour, sage, and arrange pieces of fat on top. Pour over stock or water. Cover closely, simmer till tender.

Serve hot with apple sauce made by stewing peeled and sliced apples in pan with water, pinch of nutmeg and sugar. Stew to pulp.

Pot roast may be done in a casserole in hot oven.—MISS A. CHAMBERLIN, 8 Park Drive, Hoole, Chester.

This is also an excellent method with cheaper cuts of beef, horseradish sauce taking the place of apple sauce.

POT ROAST TOPSIDE

2 lbs. topside or flank of beef.	Cooking fat.
	1 gill water.

Put meat in saucepan in which cooking fat or dripping has been made smoking hot. Brown meat top and bottom, then place joint on its sides and brown these too. Do this quickly. Pour in a gill of water or stock (using more only if necessary to save burning). Season, cover with tight-fitting lid, cook very slowly, basting frequently.

STUFFED FLANK OF BEEF

2 lbs. flank or brisket.	*For Stuffing:*
1 lb. any root vege- tables.	2 cupfuls breadcrumbs.
1 stick celery.	1 onion or leek.
Water to cover.	1 tablespoonful parsley.
A little allspice and mace.	Pinch of herbs.
	1 dried egg.
	Seasoning.
	A little milk.

Make stuffing with breadcrumbs and other ingredients (no need to reconstitute egg), mix with a little milk.

Remove inside skin from flank or bone from brisket. Spread stuffing on meat, roll, tie with string. Joint may be roasted or cooked as follows. Place in pan or casserole with sliced vegetables, spices and water to cover. Allow to simmer slowly 2 hours. Serve hot with vegetables arranged round meat with a little of liquid.

To serve cold as mock tongue, add ½ oz. gelatine to 1 gill stock, dissolve half a meat cube in it. Pour over cold joint. Press between two wetted plates with weight on top.

When remaining stock is cold, skim off fat for cooking. Thicken stock for soup by adding a cupful of oatmeal and simmering a few minutes.

THE BRAISED JOINT

2 lbs. meat (topside, flank or brisket of beef, neck of veal or neck of mutton).	Leek or onion.
	1 or 2 tomatoes.
	Herbs.
Carrots, 1 turnip.	Seasoning.
1 or 2 sticks celery.	Cooking fat.
	Water or stock.

An excellent method of cooking topside to make it more tender. Put cooking fat or dripping in saucepan, add a good layer of sliced roots, celery, chopped leek or onion, and if available, tomatoes. Season, add herbs. Put meat on top, cook in covered saucepan 15 minutes. Pour in water just to cover vegetable layer, put greaseproof paper over meat, cover pan with lid. Cook very slowly till tender, basting well.

TO MARINADE MEAT

Beef or mutton joint.	1 clove of garlic.
2 tablespoonfuls vinegar	Few peppercorns.
2 tablespoonfuls water	Pinch of mixed herbs or
1 carrot.	few sprigs fresh ones.
1 onion (optional).	

Marinading is an excellent way to treat tough or tasteless beef or mutton to make it tender and give flavour.

Put garlic, sliced raw carrot, chopped onion, herbs and peppercorns in the vinegar and water. (If liked this marinade can be brought to boil first to bring out flavour.)

Place meat in dish in which spiced vinegar, hot or cold, has been poured. Baste with liquid several times and turn. Leave not less than 2 hours, turning half time; is better if left 24 hours. Roast in usual way. Or meat may be pot roasted (*see* recipe). If any marinade is left it can be used in the gravy or saved till next required.

Another method of marinading is with salad oil. Rub meat both sides first with oil. Put a little cold vinegar in dish with pickling spice that has been crushed with a rolling pin. Put meat in marinade till next day, turning it half time. Roast in usual way.

(b) MEAT DISHES WITH VARIETY

AMERICAN HAMBURGER

½ lb. raw minced beef.	1 onion (chopped).
½ lb. sausage meat.	Seasoning.
1 teaspoonful dried egg.	

Mix beef and sausage meat with onion. Reconstitute egg with one tablespoonful water, stir into meat and season. Form into rissoles. Fry both sides till well browned. Serve as in America between buttered halves of rolls or in English fashion, with potatoes and second vegetable. Is also a useful filling for sandwich lunch.—MRS. J. E. FRY, Pentood, Tenby Road, Cardigan, Pembrokeshire, S. Wales.

BAKED RABBIT

1 rabbit.	Dripping.
1 or 2 rashers of bacon.	½ pint water.
1 onion.	Forcemeat balls
A little flour.	Seasoning.

Wash and dry rabbit. Divide into joints. Roll in seasoned flour. Melt dripping in baking tin, when hot put in prepared rabbit, chop onion finely, sprinkle over meat. Put rashers of bacon, cut in halves, on top of onion and rabbit.

Put in hot oven for 10 minutes, then lower heat to moderate and cook 30 to 40 minutes, remove rabbit from tin, put on hot dish. Sprinkle flour into baking tin and brown, adding water to make a thick gravy. Serve with forcemeat balls.

To make Forcemeat Balls

4 tablespoonfuls bread-crumbs.	½ teaspoonful mixed dried herbs.
2 tablespoonfuls chopped suet or dripping.	1 teaspoonful chopped parsley.
1 reconstituted egg.	Salt and pepper.

Mix all ingredients together, binding with egg. Bake in tin with rabbit.

BEEF MOULD

1 lb. shin of beef	A few peppercorns.
Seasoning.	Water.
2 cloves.	

An excellent mould which is not merely a wartime expedient though it makes the most of meat ration. Wash beef, simmer gently in covered pan with water just to cover, adding cloves and peppercorns. When gristle is tender, remove. Cut into small pieces, return to pan. Simmer again without lid until liquid is sufficient only to prevent burning, stirring occasionally. Season, turn into basin or mould, leave to set overnight.—MRS. A. E. SHAW, Devereux Drive, Watford.

CANADIAN HOT POT

¾ lb. stewing steak or leg of beef.	½ lb. tomatoes.
1 cabbage.	2 tablespoonfuls rice.
¼ lb. onions.	Seasoning.
Small bunch fresh herbs.	Water.

Cut meat into pieces. Wash rice. Trim cabbage. Peel and slice onions and tomatoes. Tie herbs together. Fill casserole with layers of all these, shaking rice between layers. Cover final layer with large cabbage leaves. Pour in water to come 2 inches from top. Cover closely, cook in slow oven 3 hours.

CASSEROLE OF LIVER

½ lb. liver.
1 oz. bacon.
2 onions.
Pinch of dried herbs.

2 teaspoonfuls parsley.
2 ozs. breadcrumbs.
A little seasoned flour.
¼ pint water.
A little fat.

Wash and dry liver, cut into thin slices. Dip in seasoned flour. Melt fat in casserole in oven, add liver, cook in oven with lid off a few minutes to brown. Chop bacon finely, mix with breadcrumbs, minced onions, parsley and herbs. Sprinkle this mixture over the slices of liver. Pour the water round liver, bake in medium oven.

CORNED BEEF AND BEETROOT HOT

2 thick slices corned beef.
1 cooked beetroot.
1½ cupfuls brown stock.
2 tablespoonfuls marga-
    rine or dripping.

2 tablespoonfuls flour.
1 teaspoonful vinegar.
1 teaspoonful made mus-
    tard.
Seasoning.

Melt fat in saucepan, stir in flour. Add stock. Cook till thick and velvety smooth. Add vinegar, mustard and seasoning to taste. Dice corned beef, add to sauce.

Have ready hot cooked beetroot sliced into hot pie dish; pour simmering contents of saucepan over. Serve.—Miss EVANS. Ann's Cottage, Highlands, East Horsley, Surrey.

CURRIED TRIPE

1 lb. tripe.
2 or 3 small onions.
1 dessertspoonful flour.
1 oz. dripping.
½ pint stock or milk and
    water.

1 dessertspoonful curry
    powder or 2 dessert-
    spoonfuls curry paste.
Pinch of ground ginger.
Seasoning.

Melt dripping in stew pan. When hot fry onions thinly sliced till nicely browned. Add curry powder or paste, ginger, seasoning and flour. Cook a few minutes. Then pour on stock or water and milk. Put in tripe cut into small pieces. Simmer gently fo 30 minutes. Serve with boiled rice.

HOT MEAT SLICES

Slices of cold meat.
Small onion grated.
Tiny grating of garlic.
Flour.

½ reconstituted egg.
Salt, pepper.
Breadcrumbs.
Fat for frying.

Dust slices of meat with flour. Reconstitute egg, put on plate with onion, garlic and seasoning. Coat meat with mixture, cover in breadcrumbs, fry in hot fat. Serve with tomatoes or sprouts.

HOT SPICED HAM IN TOMATO SAUCE

4 slices spiced ham.
½ lb. tomatoes or cupful of tomato sauce or puree.
½ an onion.
½ a clove of garlic.
1 bay leaf.

2 level tablespoonfuls flour.
½ cupful milk.
1 oz. dripping.
Browned breadcrumbs.
Knob of margarine.

Melt dripping in saucepan, put in finely grated onion, bay leaf and garlic, cook without browning a minute or two. Add skinned and cut up tomatoes and crush with a fork, cook with lid on 6 or 7 minutes. Blend flour with milk, stir into boiling tomato puree till it thickens. Continue stirring till flour is cooked. Remove bay leaf. If too thick add a little hot water, but coating sauce should be thick.

Put ham into heated dish, pour sauce over, sprinkle with browned breadcrumbs. Dot with margarine and brown under grill.

JUGGED STEAK

1 lb. stewing steak or skirt of beef.
1 or 2 rashers of bacon.
1 onion.
6 peppercorns.
4 cloves.
1 bay leaf.
Sprig of parsley.

½ oz. dripping.
1 oz. flour.
½ pint water.
Seasoning.
Forcemeat balls.
Redcurrant, blackberry or plum mint jelly.

Cut beef into cubes and bacon in strips. Put into saucepan, in which dripping has been melted. Fry till brown. Stir in flour and brown, add water, onion stuck with cloves, peppercorns, seasoning, bay leaf and parsley. Put lid on pan and stew very gently 1½ to 2 hours. Add forcemeat balls 15 minutes before serving. (To make balls, *see* Baked Rabbit.) Redcurrant, plum mint or blackberry jelly makes good accompaniment.

KIDNEYS AND MACARONI

2 sheep's kidneys or ½ lb. sliced ox kidney.
3 ozs. macaroni.
2 ozs. dripping or margarine.
½ oz. flour.
1 or 2 tomatoes.
1 onion.

Small piece garlic.
1 tablespoonful chopped parsley.
Good pinch mixed herbs.
Meat extract.
½ pint stock or water.
Seasoning.

Melt fat in pan. When hot fry kidneys cut into small pieces with finely sliced onion, garlic and tomatoes. When browned add flour, cook a few minutes. Then add stock or water, herbs, seasoning and meat extract. Simmer gently 1 hour. Add macaroni, cooked and drained. Cook with kidneys to heat through.

MEAT ROLY POLY

½ lb. raw minced beef.	Suet crust.
1 small chopped onion.	Seasoning.
1 teaspoonful chopped parsley.	A little thick gravy or brown sauce.
Pinch of mixed herbs.	

Mix beef, onion, herbs and seasoning with the gravy. It should not be too liquid. Roll out suet crust and spread meat mixture on it. Roll up, keeping the filling away from the edges, wrap in cloth previously dipped in boiling water and floured. Tie cloth both ends and put into boiling water. Boil 2 to 2½ hours. Alternatively it may be steamed. Serve with brown sauce or gravy and vegetables.

MUTTON MOULD

2 cupfuls cooked mutton.	Seasoning.
2 cupfuls any cooked vegetables.	Chopped parsley, lemon thyme
1 slice stale bread.	Chives or small onion.
½ pint thick white sauce.	Dash of Worcester or other sauce.

Mince mutton, bread and vegetables, mix well. Add chopped herbs, onion, Worcester sauce and seasoning; stir in white sauce, keeping mixture as thick as possible. Turn into wet mould. Turn out when cold, serve with salad or use as sandwich filling. A good way of using up tough meat and makes a little go a long way.—MRS. T. A. D. HONNOR, Church Close, Epsom.

NECK OF MUTTON WITH GREEN PEAS

1 lb. neck or breast of mutton.	½ pint shelled green peas (or tinned or soaked dried peas).
2 onions.	
1 oz. dripping.	Pepper, salt.
Sprigs of mint and parsley.	A little flour.
	Water to cover.

Cut mutton into small pieces. Slice onions. Melt dripping in a saucepan, put in meat, onions and peas. Fry a few minutes to brown. Just cover with water, add seasoning, mint and parsley chopped. Bring to boil, simmer gently 1 to 1½ hours. Thicken gravy with a little flour which has been mixed to a smooth paste with cold water.

RABBIT SURPRISE

Small rabbit.
½ pint rice.
3 tomatoes.
1 onion or 3 spring onions
1 teaspoonful salt.

½ teaspoonful pepper.
Pinch of ginger or cayenne.
1½ pints water.
Fat for frying.

Bone rabbit, cut into neat pieces, fry gently in hot fat till browned. Add salt to water, bring to boil, put in rice, boil with saucepan lid tilted for 14 minutes. Drain, stir in thinly sliced onion, sliced tomatoes, pepper and ginger. Place a little of the mixture in greased casserole with layer of rabbit on top, cover with remainder of rice mixture and half a pint of gravy. Cook gently with lid on for 1 hour.—MRS. W. E. KINSEY, Seremban, Winscombe, Somerset.

SAUSAGE PIE

1 lb. sausages.
½ lb. tomatoes, bottled or fresh.

2 onions or larger number spring onions.
Cold mashed potato.
Gravy.

Fry onions till cooked but not browned, put in bottom of fireproof dish and on them place sausages. Thinly slice tomatoes and pack round sausages. Add a little gravy. Put thick layer of mashed potato over and bake in moderate oven till sausages are cooked and potatoes well browned.—V. STOREY, Rutland Place, Boyn Hill, Maidenhead.

SAVOURY APPLES

1 cooking apple.
Cloves.

1 large sausage or 3 small ones for each person.

Take cooking apples of even size. Wipe, do not peel, core carefully. Stick clove into wall of each cavity and push in pork sausage, well pricked.

Put sausage-apples into baking dish with a little water in the base, bake slowly 20 minutes. Dish up just before apples begin to pulp and serve with any vegetables and gravy. Braised onions are good.

More sausages can be cooked round sausage-apples; in this case melted cooking fat should take place of water.—E. J. CHAMPION, Pembroke Road, Seven Kings.

SHEEP'S HEART BRAISED

2 hearts.	1½ oz. dripping.
2 onions.	1 oz. flour.
1 carrot.	¾ pint stock or water.
1 turnip.	Pepper, salt.
Bunch of herbs.	Forcemeat, as for stuffed flank.

This dish is sufficient for 4 people. Wash hearts well, remove any pipes and gristle. Dry, season with pepper and salt. Fill hearts with forcemeat. Tie piece of buttered paper over stuffing to keep in place.

Peel and cut up vegetables. Fry in the dripping, take out of frying pan and put into a saucepan. Fry hearts, put into saucepan with vegetables, adding the mixed herbs. Stir flour into fat in frying pan, brown, add stock or water. Pour gravy over hearts in saucepan. cover pan with lid, simmer gently 1½ hours

STORY OF A VEAL KNUCKLE

2½ lbs. veal knuckle.	Any available herbs—
2 rashers bacon.	parsley, thyme, mar-
Water.	joram.

Here is the story of a veal knuckle. Butcher chopped bone. Knuckle, placed in large saucepan and covered with cold water, was brought to boiling point and left to simmer gently till meat was tender. Quantity of meat was enough to make at small outlay of 1s. 6d. these two main dishes.

(1) VEAL AND BACON PIE

Make pastry. Remove meat required from knuckle, mix in bowl with chopped rashers, seasoning and chopped herbs. Put in pie dish, pour over stock from pan to about three quarters the depth of dish. Cover with pastry, cook in moderate oven till crust is light brown.

(2) VEAL MOULD

Chop remainder of veal roughly, season. Add chopped herbs. Rinse out basin with cold water, put in meat. Reduce stock in pan a little more, while still warm, pour over meat. Leave to set.—*The Daily Telegraph* HOME COOK.

(c) FISH DISHES

SIMPLE BUT OUT-*of-the*-ORDINARY

CURRIED FISH AND CABBAGE

1 cupful cooked fish, fresh, smoked or tinned
1 cupful boiled potato.
3 tomatoes chopped.
1 tablespoonful lard or cooking fat.
1 onion finely shredded.
1 dessertspoonful flour.

1 dessertspoonful curry powder.
½ teaspoonful ground spices.
1 small teaspoonful sugar.
1 saltspoonful salt.
1 cupful boiling water or fish stock.

Fry onion in fat till brown but not burned, stir in flour, mix well. Add curry powder, sugar, salt, spice, and fry gently for 10 minutes. If the mixture gets too dry add a little boiling water. Now add tomatoes and cook slowly for 10 minutes, adding gradually rest of the boiling water or fish stock and so making a thick gravy. Into this put chopped fish and potato; heat thoroughly.

Dish up in a ring of boiled rice or mashed potato. Serve with chutney and shredded cabbage parboiled and fried with flavouring of chopped onion, pepper and salt, and a few raisins or sultanas. Keep cabbage dry.—Mrs. N. COOPER, Station Hotel, Perth.

HERRING THE GREAT YARMOUTH WAY

Herring.
Seasoning.

Margarine.
2 slices of bread.

Scale herring, remove head and tail, open flat, clean, take bones out Dust slightly with fine salt and pepper.

Spread slices of bread well with margarine, put herring between. Place in hot oven, bake till well browned. Serve very hot.

This is the way my mother some 70 years ago at Great Yarmouth prepared the "long-shore" herring for breakfast or supper.—A. HAWES, Kewanee, Linksway, Northwood, Middlesex.

MACKEREL PIE

3 mackerel.
Breadcrumbs
Parsley

½ teaspoonful dried herbs.
Knob of margarine.
1 dried egg, reconstituted.
Seasoning, mace.

Remove roes. Make forcemeat with them, adding breadcrumbs, herbs, chopped parsley, plenty of seasoning, mace, margarine, beaten-up egg. Stuff fish, dot with dabs of margarine, make any remaining forcemeat into small balls and place on fish. Cover with mashed potatoes, scatter breadcrumbs over and one or two dabs of margarine. Bake 30 minutes.—*The Daily Telegraph* HOME COOK.

SAVOURY BAKED FISH

Ling, coley or other of the lesser known white fish, or fresh water fish such as bream can be used for this dish.

¾ lb. white fish.	1 onion.
1 tablespoonful grated cheese.	½ lemon or lemon essence.
2 tablespoonfuls bread-crumbs.	1 gill fresh or household milk.
Seasoning.	1 gill fish stock.
	1 dessertspoonful flour.

Steam or boil fish till tender. Flake into a baking dish and sprinkle with chopped onion, grated cheese, lemon juice or equivalent in essence, season with salt and pepper.

Mix the flour with milk and add fish stock, pour this over fish. Sprinkle over with breadcrumbs and bake in moderate oven ½ hour.— MRS. E. F. COOPER, 19 Devonshire Road, Bexhill-on-Sea.

SCALLOPS GRATINÉ

Scallops.	Breadcrumbs.
Parsley.	Pepper and salt.
Margarine.	

Remove scallops from shell and trim away beards and black portion, leaving white and yellow to cook, after washing and drying. Grease the washed and dried shell or, if preferred, small fireproof dishes with margarine. Cut up the scallops and allow about one-third quantity of breadcrumbs to that of fish. Line shells or dish with breadcrumbs, put layer of fish with plenty of seasoning and finely chopped parsley. Cover with breadcrumbs, dab with margarine and put in a fairly hot oven for ½ hour.—*The Daily Telegraph* HOME COOK.

SOUSED HERRINGS OR MACKEREL

4 herrings.	1 dessertspoonful mixed pickling spice.
1 onion, sliced.	
1 bay leaf.	1½ gills water.
1½ gills vinegar.	1 level teaspoonful salt.

Cut off heads and tails, clean, bone and fillet fish. Sprinkle each fillet with pepper and salt. Roll up with little sliced onion inside each fillet. Place in fireproof dish. Scatter pickling spice and the rest of the onion between the rolls. Add bay leaf. Pour mixed vinegar and water over fish, adding more vinegar if liquid is not sufficient to cover. Bake in slow oven 1 hour.

Fish can be done this way without boning and rolling. Remove heads and tails and clean, lay herrings in dish and add ingredients as before. Mackerel can be treated the same way.

Soused herrings are served cold; an excellent accompaniment is potato salad.

SPICED FISH SALAD

1 lb. cooked white fish.	½ pint vinegar.
6 cloves.	6 peppercorns.
2 teaspoonfuls allspice.	1 teaspoonful salt.

Remove skin from fish before putting into a deep dish. Boil vinegar and spices together for 5 minutes. Cool and pour over the fish. Let it stand for 5 hours to soak up spices during which time the fish should be basted 2 or 3 times. Turn on to a dry dish and serve with salad.— MRS. P. KYLE, Kildare, Burwash, Sussex.

TURBOT AND TOMATOES

Turbot, halibut or other white fish may be cooked in this way

1 lb. turbot or other white fish.	Seasoning.
⅛ lb. tomatoes or tomato puree.	2 teaspoonfuls mixed herbs.
1 oz. margarine.	A few breadcrumbs.

Cut turbot into cutlets or fillets, put into greased fireproof dish. Sprinkle with herbs and seasoning. Put little dabs of margarine over fish. Bake in hot oven 15 minutes.

Remove from oven. Baste. Place over fish sliced tomatoes or tomato puree. Sprinkle with breadcrumbs and dabs of margarine and seasoning. Return to oven, cook another 15 minutes.

WHITE FISH AND SPINACH CASSEROLE

1 lb. white fish.	A few breadcrumbs.
1 lb. spinach.	Dabs of margarine.
½ pint thick cheese sauce.	Seasoning.

Cook and sieve spinach. Boil fish, free it from skin and bone. Arrange layer of spinach in fireproof dish, then the fish, thirdly pour over the sauce—this is simply a thick white sauce with plenty of grated cheese stirred into it. Cover lightly with breadcrumbs, add seasoning and margarine. Reheat in oven if ingredients have been cooked the day before. If freshly cooked and still hot, put under grill to brown.— MRS. E. V. LEWIS, 1 Glenavon Crescent, Locks Common, Porthcawl, South Wales.

WHITE FISH AU GRATIN

¼ lb. white fish per person.	Anchovy or other fish paste.
Grated cheese.	A little fat.
Breadcrumbs.	Sour or fresh milk.

Wash and dry cod, haddock, or other filleted white fish. Sprinkle with salt, spread with fish paste. Put a little melted fat in oven dish, put in fish, add grated cheese and breadcrumbs. Cook ½ hour. Add a little sour milk or fresh milk soured with a few drops of vinegar, cook gently a few minutes, thicken gravy with a little flour. Serve with potatoes.—R. CROOK, Penrith, Cumberland.

(d) MEATLESS MAIN DISHES and LEFT-OVERS

BAKED CELERY CHEESE

1 head celery.	1 reconstituted egg.
6 tablespoonfuls bread crumbs.	1½ tablespoonfuls cornflour or flour.
2 tablespoonfuls grated cheese.	1 tablespoonful milk. Seasoning.
1 tablespoonful margarine.	

Cut washed celery into 2 inch lengths and boil till tender. Toast crumbs with half the margarine under grill. Grease fireproof dish, strain celery, saving the liquor, place vegetable in dish.

Make a pint of sauce as follows. Mix cornflour or flour smoothly with milk, add to remainder of margarine which has been melted in pan, cook a minute or two, remove from heat, pour in sufficient celery stock, season, return to heat and stir, cook slowly a few minutes, add egg.

Put layers of sauce, grated cheese and breadcrumbs over celery till dish is full. Bake 20 minutes in oven or brown under grill.—L. BUNYARD, Three Corners, Atlington Way, Maidstone.

GNOOCHI—CHEESE OR VEGETABLE

2 ozs. semolina.	Grated cheese.
1 reconstituted egg.	Knob of margarine.
½ pint fresh or household milk or milk and water.	Seasoning.

Heat milk, sprinkle in semolina when boiling, cook slowly till thick. Season, remove from heat, when no longer cooking stir in egg. Pour into greased shallow dish or tin so as to form a flat cake half an inch thick. When cold, cut the gnoochi in squares or fingers.

If cheese gnoochi are required, pile the fingers in greased fireproof dish. Between the layers dot margarine and sprinkle with cheese—no cheese on top. Bake in hot oven till light golden brown and serve in dish in which baked.—A. M. W., Shrewsbury.

With Vegetables

Ingredients as above

1 cupful white sauce.	Parsnip, swede.
2 leeks or onions	A few carrots.
	Pepper, salt, dry mustard.

Steam or boil vegetables while the gnoochi are being prepared. Place leeks in greased fireproof dish. Dice other cooked vegetables, place them with the gnoochi in layers on top of leeks, sprinkling each layer with grated cheese, mixed with a little dry mustard. Pour over white sauce. Sprinkle top with cheese. Heat thoroughly and brown in hot oven. Serve with potatoes baked in their jackets.—MISS G. PITT, 57 Wood Lane, Highgate.

MACARONI TOMATOES

½ lb. macaroni.	2 ozs. margarine.
½ lb. tomatoes (or tomato sauce or puree to taste).	½ teaspoonful mixed herbs.
1 minced onion.	Seasoning.
3 ozs. grated cheese	Breadcrumbs

Throw macaroni into plenty of salted boiling water. Boil rapidly about 20 minutes. When cooked, take up and drain. Melt margarine in pan, put in onion and sliced tomatoes. Add herbs. Fry till onion and tomatoes are cooked. Then add strained macaroni and cheese. Mix well. If tomato sauce or puree is used instead of tomatoes, add it with macaroni.

Turn into fireproof dish, sprinkle with browned breadcrumbs, dot with margarine, put under grill to brown.

MEAT FRITTERS

A little minced cold meat.	1 tablespoonful marga-
Grated onion.	rine.
Mixed herbs.	Seasoning.
4 ozs. flour.	1 gill lukewarm water.
1 reconstituted egg.	

Sift flour into bowl, add to it gradually the warm water and beaten egg, beat well till it is a smooth batter.

Mince meat and onion, add to batter with herbs and seasoning. Let it stand ½ hour. Melt margarine in pan. Drop spoonfuls of mixture into boiling fat. Fry till nicely brown. Remove from pan and drain.

MUSHROOM SHORTCAKE

For the Shortcake

¼ lb. flour.	2½ ozs. margarine.
4 level teaspoonfuls bak- ing powder.	Saltspoonful salt.
	¼ pint milk to mix.

Sift flour, salt and baking powder into a basin, rub in fat. Mix to stiff dough with milk. Grease sandwich tin about 6½ inches in diameter. Turn dough on to lightly floured board, shape into round. Put into greased tin, bake in fairly hot oven 25 minutes.

Filling

Mushrooms.	Cheese sauce.
Knob of margarine.	Seasoning to taste.
	Grated cheese.

Chop mushroom stalks small, stew them in a little stock, gravy or milk with seasoning and, if liked, sliced onion. Strain and use this to make thick cheese sauce.

Peel mushrooms. Melt fat in pan, add mushrooms as they are peeled, cook lightly till they have absorbed fat. Remove, chop and bind mushrooms with cheese sauce. Keep hot.

When shortcake is cooked, split in halves, sandwich prepared filling between. Sprinkle grated cheese on top and serve hot.—Miss M. Christie, Jervaulx Abbey, Ripon, Yorkshire.

PEAS AND MACARONI

1 lb. peas.	3 tablespoonfuls grated
1 cupful macaroni.	cheese.
1 tablespoonful marga- rine.	Seasoning.

Cook macaroni and peas separately in usual way. Strain and add peas to macaroni, quickly stir in margarine, cheese, seasoning. Place in dish, garnish with chopped parsley. Serve immediately. Enough for three.—H. R. Oakley, St. Crispin's Vicarage, Bermondsey, S.E.

SAVOURY PANCAKES

Pancake batter.	4 ozs. grated cheese.

Use the mixture given in pudding section for sweet pancakes, substituting a pinch of salt instead of sugar.

Just before cooking pancakes, add most of the cheese. Make fat smoking hot in pan, pour a little batter in quickly, as it sets slip knife round edges, toss or turn with knife, brown other side. Fry remaining pancakes, keeping them thin. Before folding, scatter a little grated cheese over each; fold in three.

Pancakes may also be baked. Grease saucers, pour batter into them, bake 15 minutes.

Serve with green peas, runner beans, grilled tomatoes or spinach.—MRS. FLINT, 38 Granville Road, Sevenoaks.

SCALLOPED MEAT

A little minced cold meat.
1 small minced onion or 1 tablespoonful chopped chives.
2 tablespoonfuls mashed potato.
1 dessertspoonful mushroom ketchup.

A little gravy (or meat extract and hot water).
Pepper and salt.
Knob of dripping or cooking fat.
Browned breadcrumbs.

Melt dripping in pan, add meat and onion, let it cook a few minutes. Add potato ketchup, seasoning and gravy, mix well. Grease scallop shells or individual fireproof dishes, fill with the mixture. Cover with breadcrumbs and dabs of margarine and put in good oven; bake 10 minutes.

STUFFED LEEKS

Leeks.
Meat left-overs.

1 or 2 slices bacon.
Seasoning.

Cut leeks (thick ones if possible) lengthways, leaving a little green Remove a few inside leaves from each half. Mince scraps of meat and rashers, season well. Put a layer on one half leek, also small leaves that have been removed, and place other half leek on top. Put in a little water in greased baking tin, cook gently half an hour or till tender. Serve with liquid in tin.—D. E., Golders Green.

VEGETABLE MARROW RINGS

2 small marrows or 1 medium sized one.
2 or more tablespoonfuls minced meat left-overs (cooked).
2 tablespoonfuls browned breadcrumbs.
1½ gills brown sauce or tomato sauce or gravy.

1 dessertspoonful minced onion.
1 teaspoonful chopped parsley.
Seasoning.
Small knob of margarine.

Any cooked meat or offal may be used up in this way, or cooked flaked fish may take the place of meat. Peel marrow, cut in rounds, remove seeds and lay half the rounds in a fireproof dish.

Mix minced meat, onion, parsley and seasoning. Put mixture on the layer of marrow. Cover with the rest of the marrow, pour over brown sauce or substitute. Sprinkle with browned breadcrumbs and dabs of margarine. Bake in good oven till tender.

Chapter II. VEGETABLES *COOKED and RAW*

By *The Daily Telegraph* HOME COOK

VEGETABLE cookery, rightly practised, can provide the key to much good living, particularly in this age of greater dependence on home-grown food. If methods of preparation, blending of flavours and principles of cooking are mastered, home catering will never be dull ; the housewife will have an all-the-year-round choice of appetising dishes.

Artichokes (Jerusalem)

One of the best vegetables for interesting meatless dishes. Makes *au gratin* and creamed or scalloped dishes that suggest fish in appearance. .

Asparagus

Make the most of the short-lived season. Treat asparagus by two-way plan. First asparagus of season, like all "firsts", should be served in plain fashion, and the heads eaten to the last possible inch of tenderness with melted margarine, pepper and salt or, if preferred, with a mayonnaise sauce. Left-overs yield dish for next day. Asparagus points give distinction to omelette, toad-in-the-hole or scrambled eggs, make choice sandwich filling or garnish to white fish baked with white sauce, provide out-of-the-ordinary salad and a delicious summer soup.

Beans, French and Runner

As a vegetable delicacy French are preferable to runners and less trouble to the cook, who merely washes, trims, snaps across in halves and cooks in boiling salted water till tender.

Try either variety this way : When cooked, drain, toss with margarine, add pepper and a little grated nutmeg. Serve with scrambled eggs—powdered kind.

Beetroot

Now being eaten in much larger quantities, hot as well as cold in salad, garnish or pickle form. Try other ways of serving it cold than just in vinegar. One method is to slice it thickly in a bowl, pour over creamy dressing made with fresh or dried milk, a little flour to thicken, melted margarine and seasoning. Cook a few minutes, adding a few drops of vinegar. Instead of this piquant sauce, a shredding of horse radish or onion may be added to beetroot.

Broad Beans

These call for a sauce. As a change from parsley, have cream sauce into which two tablespoonfuls of bottled tomato puree have been stirred. Caper sauce is another variation.

Celery and Celeriac

Root, stalk and leaf of celery are usable. Grate root for winter salads, mixing with equal quantity of chopped apple, a little diced beet and salad cream. Inside white stalks are best used raw in salad with their young green leaves; wash well in salted water. Use coarser leaves and stalks to flavour stews and soup. As hot vegetable, sticks may be stewed and served plain; good meatless dish is celery with tomato or cheese sauce. Celery stalk left-overs may be dipped in batter and fried as supper dish.

Celeriac may be served in the same ways as celery. Both can be scalloped, using either white sauce or breadcrumbs and margarine.

Greens

All greens, like roots and pulses, should be cooked in minimum of water and any stock used as basis for soups, sauces, stews and main vegetable dishes.

(1) *Cabbage and Savoy*: Should be halved and quartered, some of the thick stalk cut away, and a little vinegar or salt put in washing water. This will deal effectively with insects. Plunge into boiling salted water. No soda, please. 25 or 30 minutes' quick boiling is required for savoy or large cabbages—10 to 15 minutes for young summer cabbages. Some cooks add ½ teaspoonful of sugar to water. Others, considering savoys and cabbages too strong flavoured, pour away water after 5 minutes' boiling and refill saucepan with fresh boiling water.

When cooked, press greens free of all moisture. If to be served plainly, cut into small squares, sprinkle over a little seasoned oiled margarine. Stewed savoy or cabbage is appreciated. Shred coarsely, simmer very gently with 1 oz. margarine to 1 lb. green, do not add any water, cover closely with lid and cook longer than when boiled rapidly. Thicken liquid by dredging flour over, season. Other methods of cooking—stuffed with forcemeat of sage, onion and breadcrumbs; chopped and creamed with white sauce made piquant with a little vinegar and chopped gherkin; served with grated cheese scattered over; covered with white sauce, breadcrumbs and dabs of dripping or margarine and browned.

Finely shredded uncooked cabbage or savoy makes a fresh green garnish that is much in favour today for many dishes that have little or no meat. Or the shredded green provides excellent basis for spring salad when lettuce is dear, with finely chopped onion, sliced beetroot and a sprinkling of garden parsley or young mint.

(2) *Sprouts*: Should be graded for cooking; small close "buds"

may be cooked separately as accompaniment to mixed grill or garnish for a white vegetable such as celery or artichokes cooked *au gratin*.

They go well with chestnuts, the latter peeled, boiled, strained and browned in a little dripping or pounded into puree and shaped into small cakes for frying.

(3) *Spinach*: Leaves should be stripped from stems if large, and washed well. Put into saucepan with only water that clings to leaves, sprinkle with salt, boil till tender. Chop with a little margarine or top of milk and seasoning. Served with scrambled eggs, dried or fresh, this produces a main dish.

Two other spinach dishes. With white sauce, grated cheese and dabs of margarine, browned in oven. Or as puree provides stuffing for pancakes or may be stirred into equal quantity of Yorkshire pudding batter and cooked in individual dishes in oven.

Keep spinach stems. Cook them the same way as asparagus and serve piquant sauce or run margarine seasoned with pepper and salt.

Peas

Like other perfect foods, green peas are never better than when cooked in simple, straightforward way, in boiling water with sprig of mint and pinch of salt, drained when tender, tossed in saucepan with piece of margarine and a very little sugar.

They are also delicious cooked gently in margarine with young carrots, seasoned. A little water to prevent burning if needed, but the idea is for vegetables to cook in steam and their own juices. When tender dredge flour over to thicken liquid, add gradually boiling water to make sauce. Serve with new potatoes.

Left-over peas make salad with small new potatoes and sliced beetroot. Pour salad cream over or mayonnaise made with dried egg, sprinkle with chopped mint or parsley and dust of paprika or cayenne.

Roots

These provide splendid choice of dishes.

(1) *Carrots*: A dish of shredded raw carrot is served with soup, salad and some hot meatless dishes in many modern homes.

Homely North Country way of mashing equal parts of boiled carrots and turnips together with a little fat and pepper should not be forgotten. Carrots, cooked and cut into thick slices, may have melted seasoned margarine poured over and sprinkling of chervil or parsley.

(2) *Turnips*: May be creamed with white sauce or have grated cheese and breadcrumbs added to sauce and be browned under grill. They can be braised in brown sauce with parsley flavouring.

Turnip fritters are good, parboil and slice them, dip in batter and fry. Or turnips, after cooking, may be fried till crisp.

*   *   *   *   *

CABBAGE AND APPLE

1 cabbage.	Salt to taste.
1 or 2 apples.	Margarine or dripping.
1 onion or 2 shallots	1 teacupful boiling water.

Remove thick stalks of cabbage and shred as for salad. Soak in salt and water 10 minutes. Peel, core and slice apples thinly, fry thinly sliced onion or shallots in fat. Add apple to pan and when yellow add cabbage. Stir well, add boiling water, cover with lid and cook 25 minutes, or till tender; serve very hot.—H. M. I., S.W.7.

CURRIED VEGETABLES

All vegetables curry well. Have either a "green" curry, using two of the following—cabbage, cauliflower, peas and spinach—or a vegetable marrow curry or curried roots. In each case cook vegetables beforehand, chop or slice. The following recipe may be followed, substituting whatever vegetables are chosen.

2 large onions.	1 tablespoonful curry
2 carrots or swede.	powder.
1 turnip.	About ½ pint stock.
1 oz. sultanas.	Few drops lemon substi-
1 apple.	tute
Salt.	

Put dripping or other fat in pan with curry powder and sprinkling of salt. When hot add vegetables, lightly brown them, add a few sultanas or raisins if available and diced raw apple. Just cover with stock or gravy. Simmer a few minutes to bring out flavour. Just before serving add a little lemon flavouring. Serve with rice or mashed potatoes and home-made chutney.

MOCK FISH SCALLOPS OR PIE

1 lb. artichokes.	Cayenne.
Grated cheese to taste.	Seasoning.
A few breadcrumbs.	½ pint thin white sauce.
1 oz. margarine.	

Peel artichokes, put immediately into cold water containing a few drops of vinegar. Boil in salted water. Cut in pieces the size of a small oyster, arrange in greased scallop shells with breadcrumbs, margarine and seasoning. Put under grill, serve with dash of cayenne if possible.

Or put artichokes, cut up, in fireproof dish with layers of breadcrumbs and grated cheese. Pour white sauce over, finish with breadcrumbs, grated cheese and dabs of margarine. Brown in oven.

RED CABBAGE, HOT AND COLD

1 red cabbage.	1 oz. sugar.
1 small chopped onion.	1 small dessertspoonful
2 large sour apples.	vinegar.
2 ozs. margarine or drip-	Nutmeg, salt and pepper.
ping.	1 pint boiling water.

Shred cabbage, peel, core and slice apples, chop onion, put all into the boiling water to which vinegar has been added. Sprinkle with salt, pepper and a little grated nutmeg. Boil gently 1 hour, by then the water should have evaporated. Stir in sugar and margarine or dripping. Reheat and serve.

Cold left-over makes a nice salad, with addition of a little chopped onion and tarragon vinegar. Sprinkle chopped parsley over.

STEWED BEETROOT

2 teacupfuls cooked diced beetroot.	Salt, pepper.
½ pint milk, fresh or household.	A few drops vinegar.
1 dessertspoonful corn-flour or flour.	1 teaspoonful chopped parsley.
½ oz. margarine.	1 onion.

Slice and fry onion in fat. Mix cornflour or flour with a little of the cold milk, add to pan with rest of milk and seasoning. Cook five minutes to thicken sauce, stirring, add beetroot and vinegar, simmer a few minutes, serve hot with parsley sprinkled over.

STUFFED MARROW AND APPLE SAUCE

For Apple Sauce

Vegetable marrow.	½ lb. cooking apples.
Sage and onion stuffing.	½ oz. margarine.
Dabs of margarine.	1 teaspoonful sugar
	Lemon essence.

Peel marrow, cut in half, scoop out seeds, fill hollow with forcemeat. Press the two halves together and tie. Place in well greased casserole, season well, add dabs of margarine, cover with greased paper. Bake 1 hour or a little longer if marrow is large. Serve with apple sauce.

Good as an accompaniment to any hot pork dish or with sausages or sausage meat baked in same dish.—THE HOME COOK.

TOMATO PUFFS

4 oz. flour.
1 teaspoonful baking powder.
Pinch of salt.

Milk to mix.
Sliced tomatoes, fresh or bottled.

Make these to eke out the breakfast bacon. Make batter with flour, baking powder and salt mixed with milk (it should be a thick batter that will drop from the spoon).

Peel and slice tomatoes. Dip into batter, coat well. Fry puffs in the hot bacon fat till golden brown, drain and serve at once on the bacon.—MISS M. ROSS, 215 Fox Lane, Palmer's Green, N.13.

VEGETABLE PIE

This can be made with a brown sauce and pastry cover or with a cheese sauce and cover of sliced or mashed potatoes.

1: With Brown Sauce

Any vegetables in season.
½ lb. pastry.
1 oz. dripping or cooking fat.
Seasoning.

Brown Sauce
1 oz. cooking fat.
1 oz. flour.
½ pint stock or water.
Meat cube.

Some tomatoes or tomato puree should always be included, also leeks or onions. In addition any of the following vegetables are suitable— parsnips, turnips, swedes, carrots, celery, artichokes, peas, cauliflower, broad beans.

Melt fat in saucepan, add all vegetables sliced or diced, except tomatoes. Fry till browned, add sliced tomatoes, season well, cook a little longer.

Make brown sauce by adding fat to saucepan in which vegetables are cooking, stir in flour, cook till browned. Add stock or water and if required a meat cube. Allow vegetables and gravy to get cold. Put in pie dish, cover with short pastry, bake in hot oven ½ hour.

2: With Cheese Sauce

½ pint vegetable stock or water.
1 gill fresh or household milk.
1 dessertspoonful corn-flour or flour.

Pepper.
3 ozs. grated cheese.
Knob of margarine.
Cooked potatoes.

Brown vegetables as before and place in pie dish. Mix cornflour or flour with a little of the cold milk. Put stock on to boil, remove pan from fire, stir in thickening. Add rest of milk and pepper; simmer, stirring for five minutes. Just before pouring sauce over vegetables, stir into it grated cheese and margarine. Cover with sliced or mashed potatoes. Bake in oven ½ hour.

Chapter III. POTATO FARE *SAVOURY and SWEET*

MANY aspects of potato cookery have been re-discovered in the last few years. Potato pastry, cakes, puddings and tart fillings now add to the everyday uses to which housewives put this universal vegetable—first brought to England by the Elizabethans.

One point in potato cookery often overlooked is made by Soyer who gave up what he called his "fashionable culinary sanctorium" at the Reform Club to undertake a Government mission to Ireland in 1847; there are potatoes and potatoes. Some require quick boiling, others slow; some plenty of water, others little; some are best baked in their skins, others peeled.

When new potatoes are to be roasted, par-boil, remove skins, rub well with fat, dredge with a little flour, salt and pepper and finish till well browned in baking tin. That was Soyer's way.

Mashed or grated raw potato can take the place of part of the flour ingredient in suet and other steamed puddings.

AMERICAN POTATO SHORTCAKE

½ cupful riced or sieved potato.

1¼ cupfuls flour.

3 teaspoonfuls baking powder.

1 tablespoonful cooking fat.

1 reconstituted dried egg.

1 teaspoonful salt.

Milk to make light dough.

Quantities serve three people. Sift flour, baking powder and salt four times, mix thoroughly with potato. Work in fat with knife or fingers. Add egg, then milk; mix with knife as for pastry till dough leaves bowl clean. Roll out into round ¾ inch thick. Bake quickly in hot oven (if gas, at mark 8) till brown.

While hot, split, fill with mixed vegetables and serve tomato sauce separately, or vegetables may be mixed with a good sauce before inserting in shortcake. Other fillings are minced meat or fish with sauce.—D. C., Eastbourne.

CAKE OR PUDDING

¾ lb. hot mashed potatoes.

4 to 6 ozs. dripping, lard or suet or mixture.

2 ozs. sugar.

3 ozs. sultanas or other dried fruit.

Pinch of salt.

Flour to bind.

Nutmeg.

Mix a little flour with potatoes to bind, work in fat, add sultanas, sugar, salt and nutmeg. Add more flour to make fairly stiff dough.

Put in greased shallow tin, bake in slow oven till crisp and brown. Serve hot for tea or with custard as luncheon sweet.

B

CHEESECAKES

2 ozs. boiled floury potato.	1 dried egg reconstituted or same quantity made custard.
1 or 2 ozs. any dried fruit.	
1 oz. margarine.	1 tablespoonful sugar.
	Nutmeg or lemon flavouring.

Short pastry.

To make filling, whip potato to feathery white consistency with currants, sultanas or chopped raisins or dates. Add egg and sugar or if sweetened custard is used instead of egg, sugar may be omitted. Whip in lastly melted margarine and grated nutmeg or lemon flavouring.

Line patty tins with pastry, add generous layer of filling, bake in moderate oven 20 minutes.

CHOCOLATE TRUFFLES

No cooking is needed for these simple party cakes.

4 tablespoonfuls mashed potato.	2 tablespoonfuls cocoa powder.
2 tablespoonfuls sugar.	Almond or vanilla flavouring.

Mash potato thoroughly, mix in cocoa powder, sugar and flavouring to taste. Work into stiff paste, mould in balls. Roll in cocoa powder till thoroughly coated, then in chocolate vermicelli if obtainable. *Officially recommended.*

INDIAN POTATOES

2 lbs. cold boiled potatoes	1 tablespoonful curry powder.
1 large onion or sufficient spring onions.	2 tablespoonfuls dripping or cooking fat.
1 tablespoonful raisins or chopped dates.	Salt to taste.
2 reconstituted dried eggs.	Chutney or pickles.
	Boiled rice.

Place fat in large frying pan and when hot add chopped onion. When this is crisp and light golden colour, add sliced potatoes, sprinkle curry powder over, add raisins, fry 5 minutes to a light brown, turning potatoes to avoid burning. Add eggs, stir till set (in about 1 minute). Sprinkle in salt to taste. Serve with a border of rice and chutney or pickles. Enough for two persons—MRS. R. S. TISSINGTON, 8 Grove Road, Harrogate.

KENSINGTON RAREBIT

Potatoes   Cheese.
                                  Cabbage (optional).

Scrub potatoes, boil in their skins. When cooked, skin and cut into rather thick slices and put into fireproof dish, cover with very thin slices of cheese or grated cheese. Place under grill till cheese is melted and slightly brown. Serve immediately.

If cabbage, shredded, boiled in very little water and drained, is put under potato slices this will make a more complete meal.—P.B., W.8.

LANCASHIRE POTATO CAKES

½ lb. cold mashed potato.   1 teaspoonful salt.
½ lb. flour.   ½ teaspoonful baking
4 ozs. cooking fat or lard.   powder.

Mix potato, freed from lumps, with flour and rub in fat, add baking powder and salt. Roll out to ¼ inch thickness and cut in rounds with niched cutter. Bake 10 minutes in hot oven. Split open, spread with margarine.

Potato cakes are at their best eaten immediately but are very good re-heated for breakfast in frying pan with bacon.—A. L. M., County Down.

OHIO PUDDING

1 cupful self-raising flour.   ½ cupful sugar.
1 cupful grated raw potato.   Pinch of salt.
1 cupful grated raw carrot.   1 teaspoonful bicarbonate
1 cupful of any dried fruit.   of soda.

Mix all ingredients thoroughly and steam 3 hours. Juice from vegetables will bind the pudding. No milk needed.—MRS. SARGENT STOWE, Hamilton Cottage, Christchurch Hill, N.W.3.

POTATO AND LEEK SOUP

½ lb. potatoes.   Seasoning.
2 leeks.   1 pint water or stock.
½ oz. dripping or marga-   ¼ pint milk fresh or dried.
  rine.   Crisp crusts or grated
1 dried egg, reconstitu-   cheese.
  ted.

Cut up vegetables. Put them in saucepan with margarine or dripping for a few minutes with the lid on. Shake often to prevent burning.

Add stock or water. When cooked, sieve vegetables. Return puree to pan, add milk, bring to boil. Stir in reconstituted dried egg. Be sure soup is not boiling or it will curdle.

Meanwhile have bread crusts crisping in the oven. Serve in small dish with soup, or hand round grated cheese.—*The Daily Telegraph* HOME COOK.

POTATO GNOOCHI

1 cupful mashed potato.	½ cupful flour.
Gravy.	Grated cheese.

Cook potatoes, mash and use while still very hot. Turn on to pastry board, work in very quickly half a cupful of flour. Make into long roll, cut into pieces about the size of a walnut or shape in any way you please.

Have ready a saucepanful of salted boiling water. Drop in potato gnoochi, when they come to the top, draw pan to the side, let water boil gently for 10 minutes, then drain in sieve. Put gnoochi into hot dish, shake cheese over. Pour over rich gravy. Keep very hot in oven but do not let it bake. Serve with peas, beans, cauliflower or tomatoes according to season.

To make Gravy

1 small onion.	Sprig of thyme.
1 rasher of bacon.	¼ pint stock.
1 bay leaf.	1 dessertspoonful flour.

Fry onion with bacon, thyme and bay leaf. Add stock. Stir in flour, cook a few minutes. Strain.—MRS. H. DAVENPORT BROWNE, Mount Pleasant, Goudhurst, Kent.

RUSSIAN CHEESE

1½ lbs. cooked potatoes.	Breadcrumbs.
1 onion.	Margarine.
4 tablespoonfuls grated cheese.	½ pint sour milk.
	Salt, pepper.
1 dried egg.	

Chop and fry onion in margarine to golden colour. Slice potatoes, put in fireproof dish with onion. Sprinkle with breadcrumbs and grated cheese, then milk to which egg has been added. Season with salt, pepper, brown in moderate oven.—D. M. B., Chiswick.

SEVEN WAYS TO STUFF POTATOES

1 large potato per person.
2 tablespoonfuls grated cheese per person.
Small piece of margarine.

A little milk.
Pepper and salt.
Filling.

Bake potatoes in jackets. When cooked, cut off piece in middle, a little bigger than a half-crown, scoop out inside with teaspoon, put some of this into previously heated basin containing margarine and milk. Mash well with fork, add cheese, pepper and salt. Put back into potato case, leaving good sized hollow. Fill this with either : (1) scrambled egg; (2) left-over curry; (3) left-over fish flavoured with a little piquant sauce; (4) sausage meat to which a little onion and sage is added; (5) left-over mince; (6) beans in tomato sauce; (7) scrambled egg with a little chopped fried bacon.

Put potatoes back into oven to heat through. Serve very hot.— G. E. DE POMEROY, Pantile, Aldington, Ashford, Kent.

Chapter IV. PUDDINGS—PASTRIES
SWEETS THAT REQUIRE NO COOKING

APPLE SKIMMER

Apple rings.   Suet crust.

Fill a pudding basin to about an inch from brim with apple rings soaked overnight. Make light suet crust, but instead of rolling it out, pat it to thickness of about one inch. Place on top of apples, cut cross in centre to allow steam to escape. Steam rapidly 30 minutes. No cover, cloth or grease-proof paper is used in cooking this pudding and it is made without sugar, though some may be served with it.— MRS. MOORE, Coach Road, Newton Abbot.

BAKED OR BOILED CUSTARD

First method of Mixing

3 reconstituted eggs.
1 pint household milk.
1 tablespoonful sugar.

Few drops vanilla essence.
Grate of nutmeg.
Small piece of margarine.

Stir sugar into eggs, add warm milk and vanilla. Pour in fireproof dish, adding margarine flaked in tiny pieces and nutmeg on top. Stand dish in oven in tin of hot water or on asbestos mat to prevent curdling. Stir custard before it sets so that margarine is well mixed with other ingredients.

Second method

This consists of mixing egg and milk powder dry, and adding water. Substitute 5 tablespoonfuls dried milk and 1 pint water for the pint of milk.

Mix dried egg, dried milk and sugar together thoroughly, add vanilla essence and gradually the water. Pour in oven dish, add margarine and nutmeg, cook as before.

To save fuel, custard may be boiled instead of baked. A double pan is advisable, but if this is not available, put on very low gas and stir all the time. It is a good plan to put an asbestos mat under the saucepan.

BLACKCAP PUDDING (Steamed)

Soak stale bread in cold water overnight. Squeeze out water, beat well with a fork.

1 breakfastcupful bread pulp.	2 tablespoonfuls syrup.
1 breakfastcupful flour.	1½ teaspoonfuls baking powder.
1 breakfastcupful grated suet.	3 ozs. currants, dates or prunes.

Soak currants, sultanas or prunes for half an hour in warm water. If prunes or dates are used, chop them. Grease a basin, place fruit at bottom. Mix dry ingredients, make a well in centre, add syrup and milk, mix to a soft dough, beat well with a wooden spoon. Pour into the prepared basin ; it should be two-thirds filled. Cover with greased paper. Steam 2½ hours. Serve with custard or other sweet sauce.— Mrs. Wilson, 38 Western Street, Barnsley.

CHOCOLATE SPONGE PUDDING

5 ozs. self-raising flour.	3 tablespoonfuls cocoa.
3 ozs. suet (or lard or margarine).	2 teaspoonfuls baking powder.
1 tablespoonful sugar.	1 tablespoonful dried egg.
1 cupful of milk.	Vanilla flavouring.

Mix and beat dried egg with milk, flavour with vanilla. Add to dry ingredients, making a firm dough. A little more milk or water may be used if necessary. Put into greased pudding basin and steam 1½ to 2 hours.—Mrs. M. Mensinger, Oldbury Lodge, Bridgnorth, Salop.

CHRISTMAS PUDDING

(1)

½ lb. breadcrumbs.
4 ozs. flour.
4 ozs. suet or margarine.
4 ozs. sugar.
½ lb. mixed fruit.
2 ozs. peel finely chopped.
2 tablespoonfuls marmalade.

1 teaspoonful baking powder.
Milk for mixing.
2 dried eggs reconstituted.
½ teaspoonful each of cinnamon, ginger and nutmeg.

Mix dry ingredients. Add marmalade, beaten eggs and sufficient milk to mix. Steam 4 hours.—*The Daily Telegraph* HOME COOK.

(2)

2 lb. flour.
2 lb. breadcrumbs.
1 lb. shredded suet.
1 lb. sultanas or raisins.
1 lb. dates.

1 lb. apples.
8 ozs. carrots.
½ lb. golden syrup.
1 whole grated nutmeg.
6 dried eggs.
1 pint milk.

Mix flour, breadcrumbs, suet, sultanas, nutmeg. Pass apples, dates and carrots through mincing machine and add with golden syrup (can be replaced by 8 ozs. sugar). Mix dried eggs with water and add last with milk. Steam or boil 4 to 6 hours.—F. PRICE, Head Cook, King Edward VII Convalescent Home for Officers, Osborne House, East Cowes, I.O.W.

DATE CHOCOLATE PUDDING

4 ozs. fine breadcrumbs.
4 ozs. flour.
3 ozs. margarine or dripping.
2 ozs. sugar.
4 ozs. chopped dates.

2 level tablespoonfuls cocoa.
1 dried egg.
1 teaspoonful baking powder.
Milk and water or household milk to mix.

Mix breadcrumbs and flour. Rub in fat, add sugar (Demerara if possible), dates, cocoa powder, dried egg (not reconstituted) and baking powder. Stir in enough milk to make a spongy mixture. Put in greased basin, steam 2 hours.

If liked, a little ginger may be added.—K. K., London, N.21.

FOUNDATION BAKED PUDDING

½ lb. self raising flour.	1 reconstituted egg.
3 ozs. sugar.	1 gill milk.
3 ozs. margarine, suet or cooking fat.	Pinch of salt.

Sieve flour, add sugar, salt. Rub in fat, add well beaten egg and milk mix well.

Jam Pudding.—Put 3 tablespoonfuls jam at bottom of pie dish. Place mixture on top.

Fruit Pudding.—3 oz. dates, currants or sultanas, a little mixed spice. Mix with dry ingredients before adding egg.

Sponge Pudding.—Flavour with a few drops of lemon, vanilla or other essence, added to mixture last of all. Serve with jam or sweet sauce.

Bake in moderate oven 30 to 40 minutes.

FOUNDATION STEAMED PUDDING

3 ozs. flour.	½ teaspoonful baking powder.
3 ozs. breadcrumbs.	
2 ozs. cooking fat.	1 reconstituted egg.
2 ozs. sugar.	A little milk.

Mix all dry ingredients together. Beat egg, add to mixture with sufficient milk to make a dropping consistency. Beat well, put into greased basin. Cover with greased paper and steam 2 hours. Serve with sweet sauce.

Flavourings : These are added to the dry ingredients.

Chocolate	.. ..	1 oz chocolate powder or 1 dessertspoon ful cocoa powder.
Ginger	.. ..	3 tablespoonfuls treacle, ½ teaspoonful ground ginger.
Fig or date	.. ..	3 ozs. dried fruit, pinch of grated nutmeg or mixed spice.
Fruit ..	.. ..	3 ozs. currants and sultanas mixed, ½ teaspoonful mixed spice.
Marmalade or Jam	..	2 tablespoonfuls.

FRUIT-LAYER PUDDING

Any stewed fruit.	2 ozs. wholemeal flour.
2 ozs. margarine.	½ teaspoonful baking powder.
2 ozs. sugar.	
1 egg.	1 teacupful milk and water.
4 ozs. breadcrumbs.	
	Pinch of salt.

Cream margarine and sugar. Add beaten egg and mix with dry ingredients. Make a soft mixture with teacupful of milk and water.

Put a layer of mixture in the bottom of a greased dish, cover with a thick layer of any stewed fruit in season and cover with rest of the mixture. Bake in a moderate oven for 1 hour till set.—MRS. A. D. AYRE, 14 Talma Gardens, Twickenham, Middlesex.

FRUIT SHORTCAKE

1 lb. fruit pulp.	1 large cupful flour.
2 ozs. sugar.	1 teaspoonful baking
2 reconstituted eggs.	powder.

Mix flour, baking powder and sugar. Add reconstituted eggs and beat well. Fill two sandwich cake tins with mixture and bake 10 minutes in hot oven. Spread fruit pulp between as filling and dust top with sugar.—E. M. SIMPSON, 3 Harriet Walk, Knightsbridge, S.W.

HALF-HOUR APPLE DUMPLINGS

Apples.	Sugar as required.
¼ lb. self-raising flour.	Cloves.
3 ozs. suet.	A little margarine.
1 teaspoonful baking powder if plain flour is used.	Pinch of salt.

Make suet crust by shredding suet, mixing in salt, flour, baking powder if required and enough cold water to make stiff paste. Roll out. Scoop out core of each apple, fill hole with sugar and a clove, wrap crust round it.

Put each apple in a piece of greaseproof paper large enough to be able to screw round well at top. Have ready pan of boiling water. Boil half an hour. Dumplings never fail to remain in paper and are easily lifted from water. Before serving, add a little margarine and sugar to each dumpling.—MRS. C. HANCOCK, Lake Edge, Parkland Avenue, Upminster, Essex.

ORANGE RIND PUDDING

Grated rind of 1 orange.	1 tablespoonful dried egg.
8 ozs. plain flour	2 teaspoonfuls baking
2 ozs. sugar.	powder.
2 ozs. margarine.	Pinch of salt.

Cream sugar and margarine. Mix flour, dried egg in powder form, baking powder, salt ; add to creamed mixture alternately with a little water. Add grated orange rind. Pour into greased basin, steam 1 to 1½ hours.

Orange Sauce

Grated rind of 1 orange.	1 small tablespoonful
¼ pint milk.	cornflour or flour.
	Knob of margarine.
	Sugar to sweeten.

Melt margarine in pan, stir in cornflour, cook without browning a few minutes till smooth. Add milk gradually, stirring till smooth. Add sugar and orange rind. Boil a few minutes, stirring. Sufficient for 6 people.—W. N. W., Exeter.

PANCAKES

2 reconstituted eggs.	1 teaspoonful sugar
¼ lb. flour.	(pinch of salt instead if
½ pint household or fresh milk.	for savoury pancakes).

Put sifted flour in bowl with sugar, make a well, put in eggs and mix in flour gradually. Add milk by degrees, beating well all the time. Make batter ½ hour before using. Put on one side in cool place.

Heat pancake pan, rub round with, if possible, a piece of pork fat, if not available, use lard. When smoking hot, pour in a spoonful of batter. Shake pan lightly to prevent sticking, lift edges with palette knife. When browned underneath, toss on to the other side by holding pan at edge of handle and jerking lightly upwards. Just brown second side. Turn on to dish, add pancakes as they are done, keep hot.

Pancakes must be very thin. Pancake pan should be carefully wiped clean and dry after use and not washed.—LADY WILTON, Ickwell, near Biggleswade, Beds.

Pancake fillings

Instead of cut lemon and sugar, HOME COOK suggests orange or grapefruit, marmalade or apricot jam or golden syrup to which a few drops of lemon essence are added.

Undiluted lemon squash and syrup instead of sugar is an alternative. A thin layer of lemon curd is yet another idea; spread on cooked pancake before rolling.

A few sultanas also make pancake filling. Wash and pick over 2 or 3 tablespoonfuls; dry them, heat for a minute in small pan in which a scrap of margarine has been melted. Shake well. Sprinkle them on pancake before folding or rolling.

PLUM CRUMBLETOP

1 lb. plums.	1 teacupful self-raising
Margarine size of an egg.	flour.
⅜ teacupful sugar.	

Place raw plums in pie-dish with little water. Sprinkle 2 tablespoonfuls of the sugar over. Put flour in basin, rub in margarine, adding rest of sugar. The dry mixture, which should look crumbly, is sprinkled evenly and thickly on top of plums. Bake in moderate oven 30 minutes.—MRS. DUCKWORTH, 37 Broadhurst Gardens, N.W.6.

PRUNE PANCAKES

Pancake batter.
4 ozs. prunes.

Sugar (brown if possible).
Water.

Prepare pancake batter according to number to be served. Simmer prunes in water just to cover till tender, drain and stone them. Return to water in which they were cooked with a teaspoonful sugar (if liked kernels may be added). Simmer till liquid is reduced to a syrup. Sieve. Spread on each thin pancake 1 tablespoonful of this marmalade of prunes. Roll up, sprinkle with sugar, brown pancake quickly under grill.

A glass of port added to syrup is a great improvement—a hint for future reference. When prunes are returned to pan after stoning a few drops lemon juice or essence may be added.—MRS. M. MARSHALL, 21 Bulstrode Street, W.1.

RHUBARB STIRABOUT

4 ozs. flour.
1½ ozs. sugar.
Some sticks of rhubarb.

2 ozs. margarine.
Pinch of salt.
Milk for mixing.
Golden syrup for sauce.

Mix flour and salt, rub in margarine, add sugar and rhubarb cut into inch pieces. Mix with milk to the consistency of a thick batter. Bake in a hot oven for 20 to 30 minutes. Serve hot with golden syrup.— MISS C. LEITHNER, Agate, Chingford Avenue, Farnborough, Hants.

SUMMER CHARLOTTE

Cake crumbs.

Sweetened stewed fruit.
1 oz. margarine.

Grease a pie dish with margarine and spread with layer of cake crumbs about ½ inch in depth. Cover with hot, sweetened stewed fruit (preferably stoneless). Add another layer of crumbs with alternate layers of fruit, and a top layer of crumbs. Put a few dabs of margarine on top and bake in a moderate oven for ½ hour. Serve hot or cold. If the latter, turn on to a glass dish and coat with custard.—MRS. E. G. THOMAS, 8 Normanston Road, Oxton, Birkenhead.

TREACLE SPONGE

4 ozs. self-raising flour.	¼ teaspoonful ground ginger.
1½ ozs. suet.	
Pinch of salt.	1 teaspoonful sugar.
¼ teacupful golden syrup.	¼ teaspoonful bicarbonate
¼ teacupful of milk.	of soda.

Heat milk and syrup in saucepan, while cooling mix all dry ingredients, then add milk and syrup. Well beat, put in greased basin, cover with greaseproof paper and steam for 2 hours. May be served with hot custard or syrup.—Miss G. Pratchett, 60 Churchbury Lane, Enfield, Middlesex.

SWEET PASTRIES

APPLE CAKE

¼ lb. short or puff pastry.	2 ozs. sultanas or raisins.
1 lb. apples.	1 oz. margarine.
1½ ozs. sugar.	

Peel and cut up apples, stew with chopped fruit and sugar till soft. Beat in margarine when puree is ready and add, if liked, pinch of powdered ginger or cloves.

Roll out two 12-inch squares of any short or rough puff pastry, spread one with mixture. Cover with second square, press edges together, make deep cut in lattice pattern design on pastry, brush over with milk or beaten powdered egg, using 1 small teaspoonful of powder with milk. Bake in moderate oven for about ½ hour. Cut in squares.—*The Daily Telegraph* Home Cook.

APPLE SYRUP TART

½ lb. apples.	2 ozs. sugar.
4 ozs. flour.	3 cloves.
4 ozs. fine oatmeal.	2 tablespoonfuls brown
2 ozs. fat.	breadcrumbs.
Pinch of salt.	2 tablespoonfuls of golden
Water to mix.	syrup.
1 oz. sultanas or raisins.	

To make pastry, mix oatmeal, flour and salt together. Rub in fat and form into stiff paste with a little water. Roll out and line rather deep, round tin.

Peel, core and slice apples. Stew till tender in very little water with cloves. Strain off any liquid. Stir in sugar. Put mixture in pastry case and sprinkle breadcrumbs over. Cover with warm golden syrup and add sultanas. Bake in moderate oven for 30 minutes. When cold tart should be solid and carries well in a tin.—Mrs. G. Holdcroft, Alport Dairy, Alport Road, Whitchurch.

BAKEWELL TART

¼ lb. short pastry.
1 or 2 tablespoonfuls jam (raspberry for preference).
3 ozs. biscuit, cake or breadcrumbs.

1½ ozs. sugar.
1½ ozs. margarine.
1 reconstituted egg.
Almond essence.

Line shallow tin or small tartlet tins with short pastry ; cover with thin layer of jam. Spread smoothly with mixture as follows : Cream fat and sugar, add breadcrumbs, egg and almond essence to flavour well. If mixture is too stiff add a little milk. Put into hot oven, reducing heat after 10 minutes ; ready when top layer is golden brown.—*The Daily Telegraph* HOME COOK.

Another method

¼ lb. short pastry.
2 ozs. soya flour.
2 ozs. margarine.
2 dried eggs reconstituted.

1 oz. sugar.
1 tablespoonful milk
Almond essence.
Red jam.

Cream margarine and sugar, add milk and eggs, beat well. Add soya flour and lastly essence. Beat. Line tin with pastry and spread with red jam, pour filling over. Bake in hot oven ½ hour.—C. E. M., Eltham.

BANBURY TARTS

½ lb. short or rough puff pastry.
1 tablespoonful marmalade (coarse cut if possible).
3 ozs. currants or sultanas.
1 oz. sugar.

1 dessertspoonful dried egg reconstituted.
1 oz. cake crumbs.
1 oz. margarine.
Pinch of cinnamon.
Pinch of mixed spice.

Roll out pastry thinly and cut in squares or circles. Mix cake crumbs, fruit, spices, beaten egg and marmalade and add to creamed margarine and sugar. Spread mixture on half the pastry, cover with the other half. Moisten edges to keep them together. Brush over with milk and sprinkle with sugar. Bake in hot oven about 15 minutes.

BRETON PEARS

Cooking pears.
Pastry.

Sugar.

Peal and core pears, but leave them whole with little tuft of stem. Dip each in sugar and wrap in pastry. Bake not too quickly—length of time will depend on variety of pear.— *The Daily Telegraph* HOME COOK.

CURD TARTLETS

¼ lb. rough puff pastry.	1 small dessertspoonful sugar.
½ pint sour milk.	
¼ dried egg.	1 dessertspoonful sultanas or currants.
Grated nutmeg to taste.	
½ oz. margarine.	

Warm milk in pan, strain through muslin, break curd up with fork, add ingredients, lastly the egg reconstituted. Line tins with pastry, fill with curd mixture. Bake in hot oven till golden brown.—R. A., Wembley.

CUSTARD TART

¼ lb. short crust pastry.	Sugar to taste
1 dessertspoonful custard powder.	½ pint milk.
	Few drops almond essence
1½ tablespoonfuls dried egg reconstituted.	Grating of nutmeg.

Mix custard powder with a little of the milk. Boil rest of milk. Stir in custard powder smoothly, then add reconstituted egg. Stir till custard thickens, being careful not to boil. Add essence. Roll out pastry, line tin, pour custard on it, grate over a little nutmeg.

Bake in fairly hot oven ¾ hour or till slightly browned on top. Can be eaten hot or cold.

ECCLES CAKES

¼ lb. rough puff pastry.	½ oz. margarine.
3 ozs. dried fruit.	Grate of nutmeg.
1 oz. sugar.	

Roll out pastry thinly, cut into square of about 3½ inches, spread thinly with ingredients which have been mixed together. Fold over, press edges together, slash top, brush over with white of egg or sugar and hot water. Bake in hot oven 15 to 20 minutes.—*The Daily Telegraph* HOME COOK.

FRUIT FLAN

Short crust.	Stewed fruit.

For Syrup

¼ pint juice from stewed fruit (slightly sweetened).	2 ozs. sugar.
	1 teaspoonful cornflour or arrowroot.

Line a flan case or deep sandwich tin with pastry. Prick pastry at bottom of tin and bake. When cold fill with cooked strained fruit—

almost any variety may be used, apples, raspberries, plums, gooseberries and so on.

Make syrup by mixing cornflour or arrowroot with a little cold fruit juice and adding sugar. Bring the rest of the fruit juice to boil, pour on to cornflour, boil quickly till transparent. Pour syrup over fruit in flan and leave till cold.

Syrup may be made with gelatine instead of cornflour. Heat fruit juice and sugar, dissolve one level teaspoonful gelatine in it. When cool but not set pour over fruit. Leave to set. A few drops of colouring may be added to increase the attractive appearance of this sweet.

GINGER TARTLETS

¼ lb. short pastry.	1 dessertspoonful golden
4 ozs. rolled oats.	syrup.
1½ ozs. margarine.	1 small teaspoonful
1½ ozs. sugar.	ground ginger.

Bring margarine, ginger, sugar and golden syrup to the boil. Remove from heat and stir in rolled oats. Fill small patty tins lined with pastry and bake in moderate oven 20 minutes.—MRS. C. S. HEATHER, 12 Linwood Road, Bournemouth.

PRUNE AND APPLE TART

½ lb. short pastry.	½ lb. prunes.
¼ pint custard.	½ lb. apples.

Roll out pastry fairly thinly and put in round flat tin about 1½ inches deep. Put a layer of puree of prunes (stewed and sieved), a layer of custard, and a layer of apples cut in thin slices and arranged nicely in rings. Bake about 30 minutes till apples are golden brown.—M., Sydenham.

PUMPKIN PIE

½ lb. short pastry.	1½ tablespoonfuls sugar.
Ripe pumpkin sufficient	Ginger or nutmeg to
to yield 1 lb. of sieved	flavour or equal quanti-
puree.	ties of both.
1 oz. margarine.	1 gill of milk.
1 egg.	

Peel and remove seeds and pith from pumpkin. Boil gently in water till soft, strain and rub through sieve. Work in margarine, sugar, flavouring, yolk of egg and milk. Line pastry case, fill with mixture and bake lightly. Whisk white of egg with a little sugar, pile on top of puree and return to oven for meringue to set.

If liked, white of egg can be omitted and pie covered instead with pastry. In this case mix ingredients with reconstituted egg.—*The Daily Telegraph* HOME COOK.

RHUBARB FLAN

⅛ lb. short pastry.	1 teaspoonful corn-
1 lb. rhubarb.	flour.
2 ozs. sugar.	Few drops cochineal
¼ pint water.	(optional).

Line flan case with pastry rolled out thinly. Dissolve sugar in water and boil. Cut rhubarb into 2½ inch lengths, and poach carefully in this syrup. Cool and place pieces on cooked flan case, forming the spokes of a wheel. Heat the syrup and thicken with cornflour. Add cochineal, stir until nearly cold, then pour over rhubarb.—MISS H. ROBINSON, 4 Amberleaze Drive, Pembury, Kent.

Recommended with early forced rhubarb.

COLD SWEETS

APPLE TRIFLE

Fingers of plain cake.	Few drops pink fruit
1 lb. cooking apples.	colouring.
½ pint custard.	Sugar.
½ teaspoonful powdered	Biscuit crumbs.
gelatine.	Bottled strawberries.

Fruit in season may take the place of apple. Line glass dish with cake fingers. Cook apples with sufficient sugar till tender and add colouring. Sieve. Cover fingers with some of the apple puree, continue with alternate layers of cake fingers and puree.

Add gelatine dissolved in a little hot water to custard. Whisk custard well, put on top of trifle. Sprinkle with grated sweet biscuit crumbs and decorate with a few whole bottled strawberries if available.

CHOCOLATE CREAMS

Dried milk.	½ teaspoonful flavouring
1½ ozs. margarine.	(vanilla, orange, al-
1½ ozs. castor sugar.	mond or coffee).
1½ ozs. chocolate powder	3 tablespoonfuls hot
or cocoa.	water.

Beat sugar and margarine together. Melt chocolate in hot water, beat well into creamed mixture. Then work in powdered milk (not reconstituted) till mixture is consistency of thick cream. Lastly add flavouring. Fill individual glasses with the cream ; serve very cold with biscuits or fingers of cake.

CORNISH TRIFLE

1 pint milk.
3 level tablespoonfuls ground rice or semolina.
2 tablespoonfuls sugar.
Almond essence.

½ oz. cocoa.
Cake or biscuit crumbs.
1 tablespoonful marmalade or jam.

Put milk, cocoa, ground rice (or semolina) and sugar in saucepan and bring to boil, stirring all the time till thickened. Have ready dish in which it is to be served with layer of crumbs, topped by the jam or marmalade. Flavour the mixture in the pan and pour over crumbs while still hot. Put aside till cool.—Mrs. ARCHER, Bramble Cottage, St. Agnes, N. Cornwall.

DEVON WHISK

½ pint thick sour milk.
1 level tablespoonful raspberry jam or stewed raspberries.

1 dessertspoonful sugar.
1 white of egg or same amount of custard.

Hang sour milk in muslin till whey drains away and only thick curd is left. Add sugar, raspberry jam or pulp and lightly beaten white of egg or custard. Whisk all well together, serve in glass dish.—D. M. B., Chiswick.

FRUIT WHIP

¼ pint fruit juice, syrup from tinned fruit or jam diluted with a little hot water.

¼ pint hot water.
4 level teaspoonfuls powdered gelatine.

Melt gelatine in hot water and when dissolved add fruit juice. Mix together and put to set in cool place. If well whipped for 15 minutes when nearly cold it gets foamy and nearly doubles in quantity. Jelly may then be put in individual glasses to finish setting.—G. A., Shiplake Row.

MARROW COMPOTE AND JUNKET

1 small vegetable marrow.
½ teacupful sugar.

1 teacupful cold water.
1 teaspoonful ground ginger.

Put water, sugar and ginger into saucepan, boil for a few minutes until it becomes slightly syrupy. Peel marrow, remove seeds, cut into pieces the size of a small egg, add to syrup in pan, and bring to boiling point, then simmer until transparent. Eat cold with junket.—Mrs. J. G. SAMSON, Ayres End, Kersey, Hadleigh, Suffolk.

MEXICAN CHOCOLATE WHIP

1 tablespoonful chocolate powder or cocoa.
2 tablespoonfuls semolina.
1 pint water.
Vanilla essence.

2 tablespoonfuls coffee essence.
1 tablespoonful and 1 teaspoonful sugar

Heat 1 tablespoonful water and 1 tablespoonful sugar till caramelled. Pour on remainder of pint of water and boil. When boiling sprinkle in semolina and continue to boil 5 minutes. Mix teaspoonful of sugar with chocolate powder and coffee essence and add to mixture in saucepan. Boil 5 minutes. Pour into basin, add teaspoonful vanilla essence. Whip with whisk until mixture is light. Pile in glasses and top with chocolate powder and mock cream.

PEAR CONDÉ

Cold boiled rice
Mock cream.
Fruit juice.

Any fruit, but pear, peach or apricot best.

Put rice into individual glasses, add fruit and a little of the juice of syrup. Finish with mock cream.—*The Daily Telegraph* HOME COOK.

SUNSET MOUSSE

1½ tablespoonfuls raspberry or strawberry jam.
Plain sponge fingers or biscuits.

Small tin thick milk.
⅛ teaspoonful powdered gelatine diluted in 1 teaspoonful warm water.

Add diluted gelatine to milk; then add jam and whisk. Pile in individual glasses, forking top to give rocky effect. Plain sponge fingers or biscuits accompany this sweet.

VANILLA ICE CREAM

1 pint milk.
1 tablespoonful custard powder.
3 tablespoonfuls sugar.

2 reconstituted dried eggs.
⅜ tin liquid evaporated milk.
2 drops vanilla essence.

Make custard in usual way with the pint of milk, custard powder and sugar. Stir in well beaten dried eggs, being careful not to let it boil. Allow mixture to cool.

Whisk five minutes, adding vanilla essence.

Pour into freezing tray, turn to cold control No. 6. When starting freeze round the edges, remove tray from refrigerator, scrape the frozen part round the edges, beat it well into mixture. Put tray back, repeat this process two or three times till the whole mixture is the same consistency. This beats a lot of air into the ice cream.

At the last beating add the evaporated milk, whip mixture till light and frothy. Replace tray in refrigerator, turn cold control to No. 4, leave one hour. Turn cold control to No. 2, leave till wanted.—D. E. D., Pinner.

VANILLA ICE CREAM (Another Method)

Large tin of unsweetened liquid evaporated milk.	2 teaspoonfuls powdered gelatine.
Sugar or sweetened condensed milk to flavour	½ teacupful hot water.
	Vanilla essence.

Dissolve gelatine in hot water and allow to cool. Pour tinned milk into bowl and stir in cool gelatine. Sweeten with sugar or sweetened condensed milk and flavour with a few drops of vanilla essence. Place bowl (covered) in bottom of refrigerator to cool thoroughly, then thoroughly whisk and pour into ice trays. If ice-cream is required within short time, turn indicator to "maximum", but if three hours are to elapse, normal setting will do. Those with no refrigerator will enjoy the whisked cream with fruit.—MRS. K. W. ROSE, 2 Montolien. Gardens, S.W.15.

CHAPTER V. SAUCES *SWEET and SAVOURY*
—FILLINGS—MOCK CREAMS

APPLE CURD SAUCE

1 lb. apples.	1 tablespoonful sugar.
4 cloves.	1 tablespoonful water.
1 tablespoonful golden syrup.	Few drops rum essence or 1 tablespoonful rum
Few drops lemon essence	or sherry.
Grate of nutmeg	½ pint custard

Peel and core apples and stew for few minutes in water with cloves. Add sugar and syrup and stew till apples are soft, stirring all the time. Remove cloves and when cool stir in the custard to which lemon essence and nutmeg have been added. Mix apple pulp and custard well together, adding the rum or sherry.—E. S., Eastcote.

This is a good Christmas pudding sauce. It may also be used as accompaniment to most steamed puddings.

CHOCOLATE CUSTARD SAUCE

½ oz. custard powder.
¼ oz. cocoa powder.
Few drops vanilla essence

½ pint milk.
½ oz. sugar.

Mix custard, cocoa and sugar, blend with a little cold milk. Bring remainder of milk to boil, remove from pan, pour on cocoa mixture stir well. Return pan to heat and simmer 3 or 4 minutes. Add vanilla.

CHOCOLATE SAUCE

½ oz. margarine.
½ oz. flour.
½ oz. cocoa powder

½ pint household or fresh milk.
½ oz. sugar.
Few drops vanilla essence.

Mix flour, cocoa and sugar in basin. Melt margarine in saucepan, add mixture. Cook slightly without browning, add milk gradually, stir constantly till boiling. Reduce heat, simmer 3 or 4 minutes. Add vanilla.

CUSTARD SAUCE

1 dessertspoonful flour.
1 dessertspoonful sugar.
Few drops of vanilla essence.

1 dessertspoonful dried egg.
½ pint milk.

Mix flour, dried egg and sugar with a little milk to make a cream. Boil remainder of milk and pour on to mixture, stirring. Return to saucepan, boil for 5 minutes, stirring, until sauce thickens. Add flavouring.

FOUNDATION WHITE SAUCE

1 oz. margarine.
1 oz. flour.
½ pint milk, fresh or household.

½ oz. sugar, or if for savoury dish, seasoning.

Melt margarine in saucepan. Stir in flour and cook a minute or two without browning, stirring. Add a little of the milk and stir until smooth. Add the remainder of the milk, stirring all the time over low heat, until sauce is the consistency of thick cream. Sweeten or add seasoning.

This makes a plain white sauce or may be varied in the following ways.

Savoury

Anchovy	..	add 2 teaspoonfuls anchovy essence.
Cheese	..	add 1½ oz. grated cheese.
Onion	..	add 2 onions boiled and chopped.
Parsley	..	add 1 dessertspoonful chopped parsley.

In each case stir flavouring addition into sauce when ready to serve and heat again.

Mustard.—When making white sauce stir 1 good teaspoonful mustard into flour before putting it into pan. After cooking add a few drops of vinegar.

Sweet

Flavourings are added when sauce is made.

Chocolate	..	1 tablespoonful melted chocolate or 1 dessert-spoonful cocoa.
Coffee ..	..	essence to taste.
Spiced ..	..	pinch of mixed spice, nutmeg or cinnamon.

Vanilla or other essence, orange, ratafia, almond, etc.—a few drops.

GREEN TOMATO CREAM

6 medium-sized green tomatoes.
¼ pint milk.
Salt and pepper.

1 teacupful fresh parsley leaves.
1 dessertspoonful corn-flour.

Put through a mincer tomatoes and parsley. Mix cornflour to a smooth paste with a little of the milk. Boil remainder of milk and pour on to cornflour, stirring all the time. Turn cornflour and minced tomatoes and parsley in to a double saucepan, add salt and pepper to taste, and simmer all until it thickens. Pour over fish or vegetable dish.—MRS. P. MACNEILL, 4 Paget Road, Stoke Newington, N.16.

HARD SAUCE

1 oz. butter or margarine.
1 oz. soft sugar. (preferably brown).

Flavouring—ground ginger, grated nutmeg or cinnamon.

Beat together margarine and sugar ; add flavouring and beat again.

INDIAN MINT CHUTNEY (Uncooked)

This variation of the usual mint sauce is delicious with cold meat.

1 good handful fresh mint leaves.	1 tablespoonful sugar.
1 teaspoonful chopped onion or chives.	Salt, pepper to taste. 2 tablespoonfuls vinegar.

Put mint and onion or chives through mincing machine. Add other ingredients. Mix well.—MISS H. HARDING, Little Shaw, Dorking.

SALAD CREAM (For Immediate Use)

1 tablespoonful dried milk.	¼ teaspoonful made mustard.
A little water.	⅛ teaspoonful sugar.
Pepper and salt to taste.	1 teaspoonful vinegar.

Mix dried milk to a paste with a little water, then add other ingredients and mix well.—MISS DOROTHY PETTERS, Arnewood Hotel, Bournemouth.

THIN JAM SAUCE

2 tablespoonfuls any jam.	Few drops of lemon essence.
1 gill water.	

Put jam and water into pan. Bring to boil. Boil a minute or two. Remove from heat. Add lemon essence and serve.

TOMATO SAUCE

¼ lb. tomatoes.	1 level teaspoonful sugar.
½ carrot.	1 oz. margarine or dripping.
1 onion.	
¼ stick of celery.	1 oz. flour.
Sprigs of thyme and parsley.	½ pint stock or water.
1 bay leaf.	Salt and pepper.

Put dripping in pan, when hot add sliced onion, tomatoes, celery, carrot, herbs and sugar. Simmer over very low heat with lid on for half an hour. Remove and rub through sieve. Season.

Mix flour with a little cold water. Return tomato puree to pan, add stock, then thickening, bring to boil, simmer 2 or 3 minutes.

This is a useful sauce with macaroni, rice, mince or sausage meat.

FILLINGS

CHOCOLATE

3d. block of plain chocolate.	2½ ozs. margarine.
Boiling water.	

Dissolve chocolate over a basin of boiling water. Cream margarine and mix well with chocolate. Leave until cold, when it will thicken and set. Spread over cake or between sandwich.—M. G., Watford.

CHOCOLATE BUTTER

1 teaspoonful margarine.

2 tablespoonfuls chocolate or 1 dessertspoonful cocoa.

2 teaspoonfuls castor sugar.
Black coffee or milk.
Few drops vanilla (if milk is used).

Cream margarine and sugar and add cocoa. Mix with enough black coffee to make mixture pliable for spreading. If preferred, mix with milk flavoured with vanilla essence to taste.—M. B., Wembley.

CHOCOLATE SPREAD

(1) UNCOOKED

1½ teaspoonfuls cocoa.
1 oz. sugar.
1 oz. margarine.

1 teaspoonful coffee essence.

Cream together the margarine and sugar till light and fluffy. Work in the cocoa, last of all stir in the coffee essence and beat again.

(2) COOKED

1 teacupful milk.
1 tablespoonful cocoa.
Small lump of margarine.

1 tablespoonful custard powder.
1 tablespoonful sugar.

Mix together custard powder, sugar and cocoa with very little cold milk. Put margarine in saucepan with rest of milk, when boiling pour on to cocoa mixture and return to pan. Boil till thick, stirring all the time.

FRUIT CREAM

Small tin condensed milk.
¼ cupful fruit—stewed or fresh soft fruit.

Lemon flavouring.

Add lemon flavouring to condensed milk and beat till it thickens. Fold in fruit—if apple, stew as dry as possible, with flavouring of clove, nutmeg or cinnamon. In season raspberries or strawberries may be used uncooked.—E. M., Bideford.

MARZIPAN

(1)   2 ozs. soya flour.
1 oz. margarine.
1 tablespoonful water.

2 ozs. sugar.
1 small teaspoonful almond or ratafia essence.

Put margarine and water in saucepan; boil up. Remove from heat, add essence and sugar, stir well, add soya flour. Knead all well together till free from cracks.

As strength of essence varies, it is best to add a few drops at a time and taste.

(2) 2 tablespoonfuls peanut butter.
1/2 teaspoonful almond essence.

1 tablespoonful margarine.
2 tablespoonfuls sugar.
Breadcrumbs.

Beat fats and sugar well together to creamy consistency, add gradually enough breadcrumbs—made pale golden brown on oven sheet or under grill—until kneading consistency. Lastly add almond flavouring.

MOCHA FILLING

1 tablespoonful strong coffee essence.
2 ozs. margarine.

1 oz. castor or granulated sugar.
1 oz. powdered or grated block chocolate or cocoa.

Gently melt margarine, sugar and chocolate (must not boil). When well blended beat in coffee essence. Makes delicious filling for sponge or chocolate cakes, or when set a kind of fudge is available.—Mrs. G. BALLARD, Silverthatch, Hordle.

MOCK CREAMS

MOCK CLOTTED CREAM (Cornflour Method)

1/4 pint milk.
1/2 oz. cornflour.
2 ozs. margarine.

1/2 oz. sugar.
3 to 4 drops vanilla essence.

Blend cornflour with a little cold milk until it forms thin cream. Bring rest of milk to boiling point and pour on to cornflour. Stir thoroughly till free from lumps, return to pan and cook gently 5 minutes, stirring all the time. Pour into basin, leave till cold.

Cream margarine and sugar together, beat in cold cornflour mixture very gradually and thoroughly with small wooden spoon. Mixture will gradually become light and fluffy. Add vanilla with last spoonful of cornflour. The more the mixture is beaten the thicker or more clotted it becomes. Instead of vanilla, cream can be flavoured with cocoa or coffee essence.—B., Hartley-Wintney.

DRIED MILK METHOD (1)

1 tablespoonful dried milk.
2 ozs. margarine.

1 teaspoonful sugar.
Few drops of vanilla essence.

Beat margarine and sugar together. By degrees add dried milk. Flavour with vanilla and beat until very smooth.—E. M. K., Worthing.

DRIED MILK METHOD (2)

Dried milk.
3 teaspoonfuls sugar.
Margarine size of a walnut.

3 teaspoonfuls boiling water.
Essence to flavour.

Mix sugar, boiling water and margarine together until dissolved and then add dried milk gradually, stirring all the time, until desired thickness is obtained. Do not make too thick as it will thicken when cold. Add flavouring essence last—vanilla is good.

QUICK MOCK CREAM

This gives the finishing touch to any individual sweet.

Half teaspoonful powdered gelatine diluted in a teaspoonful of warm water, added to contents of small tin of evaporated liquid milk and well whisked, makes ample supply of mock cream.

Chapter VI. CAKES of TODAY

ALMOND-OATMEAL FRUIT CAKE

6 ozs. self-raising flour.
4 ozs. fine oatmeal.
3 ozs. margarine.
1 oz. lard or shredded suet.
3 ozs. sugar.

1 egg (fresh or reconstituted).
3 ozs. sultanas or dates.
10 drops almond essence.
1 small cupful of milk.

Rub fats into mixed flour and oatmeal; add sugar and fruit. Beat egg and add to dry ingredients. Add almond essence to milk, then stir into cake mixture slowly. Beat well. Pour into 7-inch cake tin and cook in a moderate oven for 1 hour 10 minutes.

AMERICAN FOUNDATION CAKE

1½ cupfuls plain flour.
2 small teaspoonfuls baking powder.
⅔ cupful of milk.
¼ cupful sugar.

½ teaspoonful salt.
1 dried egg (reconstituted).
3 tablespoonfuls melted fat.

Sift dry ingredients together. Mix prepared egg, milk and fat together and add to dry ingredients to get dropping consistency. Pour into greased tin, cover with this topping.

1 tablespoonful margarine.

⅛ teaspoonful ground cinnamon.

1 tablespoonful sugar.

2 tablespoonfuls dry breadcrumbs.

2 tablespoonfuls sifted flour.

Cream margarine and sugar, add cinnamon, flour and crumbs. Mix to consistency of coarse crumbs. Cover cake and bake in moderate oven about 45 minutes.

Without the topping this cake is a good foundation cake to which the housewife can add flavouring as desired. This recipe comes from the U.S.A.—Mrs. F. Eaton, 102 Firtree Road, Banstead, Surrey.

AMERICAN GINGERBREAD

1 teacupful dark treacle or golden syrup.

2¼ teacupfuls flour.

4 ozs. margarine and cooking fat mixed.

1½ teaspoonfuls ground ginger.

¼ teaspoonful salt.

¼ teacupful boiling water.

1 teaspoonful bicarbonate of soda.

1 teaspoonful mixed spice.

Melt fats in boiling water, add treacle to which soda, dissolved in a little milk has been added. Mix all dry ingredients thoroughly. Stir liquid mixture, and whilst bubbling pour into dry ingredients. Beat well. Pour into greased shallow tin, bake slowly 45 minutes.—Miss M. Quartermaine, Little Croft, Luddington Avenue, Virginia Water.

BOILED FRUIT CAKE

½ lb. self-raising flour.

4 ozs. golden syrup or 2 ozs. syrup and 2 ozs. sugar.

4 ozs. dried fruits (a few chopped dates if available).

3 ozs. any form of cake-making fat.

1 teacupful milk and water.

1 teaspoonful mixed spice.

1 teaspoonful ground ginger.

1 teaspoonful bicarbonate soda.

Boil all ingredients together, except flour and bicarbonate of soda, for 3 minutes. Set aside and when mixture is almost cold, stir in the flour to which the bicarbonate of soda has been added. Bake in a moderate oven 2 hours. Keeping for a few days before cutting improves this cake.—Mrs. D. Genge, The Gables, Tisbury, Wilts.

BOSTON BREAD

2 cupfuls national flour.
2 cupfuls wholemeal flour (or 4 cupfuls national flour).
1 teaspoonful salt.
1½ teaspoonfuls bicarbonate of soda.

1 cupful golden syrup.
2 cupfuls fresh milk.
2 teaspoonfuls baking powder.
1 egg, fresh or reconstituted.

Mix golden syrup and 1 cupful of milk in a bowl. Sift together flour, baking powder and salt and add to syrup mixture in bowl. Mix bicarbonate of soda in the second cupful milk and add to other ingredients. Lastly add well-beaten egg.

Beat the whole mixture vigorously. Line 4 upright cylindrical tins with greased paper. , These should be slightly larger than household milk or dried egg tins. If only these tins are available, use six of them. More than half fill them, place lid on firmly. Lids must fit on the outside; tins with inner rims at the top are useless, as the bread could not be got out. Place tins in very large saucepan half filled with boiling water and cover pan. Steam 3½ hours. Remove tins from water, take off lids. After a few minutes reverse tins and shake bread out and stand on wire to cool. Cut in round slices and butter. It is best eaten the next day, and is excellent up to 4 or 5 days. **Keep in** dry tin with lid on.—P. W., Shaldon.

A cupful of dried fruit—dates, raisins or sultanas may be added.

CHOCOLATE FRUIT CAKE

½ lb. self-raising flour.
Pinch of salt.
1 small tablespoonful golden syrup.
3 ozs. raisins, sultanas or dates.
½ teaspoonful vanilla essence.

4 ozs. margarine
3 ozs. sugar.
1 oz. cocoa powder.
2 reconstituted eggs.
1 tablespoonful milk

Sieve flour into basin, with salt, sugar, fruit and cocoa. Rub in fat. Dissolve syrup in warmed milk. Make a well in flour mixture, pour in beaten egg, syrup and vanilla essence.

Blend mixture thoroughly. Put into greased cake tin and bake in moderate oven 1 to 1¼ hours.

Chocolate Covering

2 dessertspoonfuls cocoa.
1 oz. margarine.
2 teaspoonfuls sugar.
Vanilla essence to taste.

1 dessertspoonful dried milk powder.
2 tablespoonfuls water.

Put ingredients, except essence, into small saucepan. Heat slowly, stirring till smooth. Add essence, spread mixture over cake and leave to set.

CHRISTMAS CAKE

(1)

12 ozs. plain flour.
10 ozs. fat (half margarine, half lard).
6 ozs. sugar.
1 lb. mixed cake fruit.
2 eggs, shell or reconstituted.
1 teacupful milk.

A little candied peel (if available).
A little powdered spice (optional).
Pinch of ginger.
½ teaspoonful bicarbonate of soda.

Cream fat and sugar, add fruit, peel, spices, flour, then well-beaten eggs, and lastly milk with soda dissolved in it. Bake in paper-lined tin for three hours in a slow oven. Keeps two months.—MRS. F. C. MOLESWORTH, Culforth, Bideford.

(2)

½ lb. self-raising flour.
2 dried eggs reconstituted.
½ lb. mixed dried fruit.

¼ lb. margarine.
¼ lb. sugar or 2 tablespoonfuls treacle.
A little milk.
Pinch of salt.

Melt fat, beat well, add sugar or treacle, add well-beaten eggs, gradually alternating with flour, with which salt has been sifted, adding milk till dropping consistency. Beat well, stir in dried fruit. Bake 1½ hours in moderate oven.

To ice, beat together cupful sugar, 2 tablespoonfuls margarine. 2 tablespoonfuls liquid milk, ½ teaspoonful vanilla essence. Place on top. Decorate with small artificial flowers.—K.J.O., Sutton-in-Ashfield.

CINNAMON CREAM SPONGE

1 good dessertspoonful margarine.
1 tablespoonful golden syrup.
4 oz. self-raising flour (or plain flour and 2 heaped teaspoonfuls baking powder).

4 ozs. sugar.
1 dried egg reconstituted.
¼ cupful milk (household milk will do).
½ teaspoonful bicarbonate of soda.
2 teaspoonfuls cinnamon.
Pinch of salt.

Cream margarine and sugar thoroughly. This gives good even texture. Add egg, beat well. Add syrup, mix it in well. Sift together flour (baking powder if required), salt and cinnamon. Dissolve soda in milk. Add these two mixtures alternately to egg mixture to make a very soft dough. Pour into two 7-in. sandwich tins, bake in moderate oven about 20 minutes.

Put the two halves together with jam, syrup, or prepared chocolate mixture, or with mock cream made with margarine and sugar and a little boiling water beaten together.—T. P., Edinburgh.

COFFEE CAKE

3 ozs. sieved flour.
1 oz. cornflour.
4 ozs. margarine.
4 ozs. sugar.
1 large teaspoonful baking powder.

2 dried eggs (reconstituted).
1 small teaspoonful vanilla essence.
1 tablespoonful strong coffee, warm.
2 ozs. chopped nuts (if available).

Cream butter and sugar, sift flours and baking powder together, adding nuts. Whisk eggs well and add to them the warm coffee and vanilla. Add flours and egg mixture alternately to the fat mixture, beating all the time till well mixed. Bake in moderate oven 50 minutes to 1 hour. When cold cut through centre and sandwich together with:

Coffee Nut Filling

2 ozs. castor sugar, 1 oz. margarine, 1 teaspoonful strong coffee, ½ teaspoonful vanilla essence. Beat margarine and sugar to a cream and add essences and sufficient ground nuts (biscuit crumbs or fine breadcrumbs may be substituted) to make mixture of a spread consistency.—MRS. A. CAMPBELL HOLMS, Michael's Fold, Grasmere, Westmorland.

COUNTRY HOUSE CAKE

12 ozs. flour.
3 ozs. sugar.
4 ozs. margarine.
1 teaspoonful bicarbonate of soda.
1 teaspoonful mixed spice

6 ozs. raisins or other dried fruit.
1 teaspoonful baking powder.
½ pint warmed milk.
1 teaspoonful cinnamon.

Cream margarine and sugar together and add dry ingredients which have been well mixed. Stir in warmed milk, beat well. Bake in a moderate oven about 2 hours.—*The Daily Telegraph* HOME COOK.

HOT CROSS BUNS

1 lb. flour.
4 ozs. lard or margarine (or mixture of both).
2 ozs. sugar.
2 to 4 ozs. currants or sultanas.

Small teaspoonful mixed spice.
1 oz. yeast
Pinch of salt.
Household milk to make soft dough.

Put dry ingredients (keeping back a little sugar) into warm bowl, rubbing in fat, and mix thoroughly, making well in centre. Cream yeast with remaining sugar and milk made warm. Add to flour, mix well. Beat thoroughly into smooth, soft dough and leave in warm place to rise, about 1½ hours.

Roll out, cut or shape into small rounds, mark with cross, brush over lightly with beaten dried egg and milk or milk alone. Leave to rise in a warm place 15 minutes on greased oven sheet or flat tin. Bake 15–20 minutes in quick oven.—*The Daily Telegraph* HOME COOK.

PAN MUFFIN

4 tablespoonfuls flour.
1 tablespoonful household milk.
1 tablespoonful dried egg.
1 teaspoonful salt.
½ teaspoonful bicarbonate of soda.

½ teaspoonful cream of tartar.
Frying fat.
Water to mix to thick batter (about 6 tablespoonfuls).

Mix all but the soda and cream of tartar after breakfast and put in cool place. Twenty minutes before tea beat soda and cream of tartar into mixture. Grease a thick frying pan with dessertspoonful fat and pour in the batter when hot. Slip palette knife under cake, and when it sets lower heat a little. Brown underside, turn, adding more fat if pan is dry. Lower heat, cook for a few seconds to dry through. Cut in four, serve hot with margarine.—L. FRANCES, 6 Boscobel Road, St. Leonards-on-Sea.

PINK LAYER PARTY CAKE

1 cupful self-raising flour.
½ cupful pink blancmange or pudding powder.

¼ cupful sugar.
2 oz. margarine.
2 dried eggs reconstitued in milk.

Beat sugar and margarine together. Mix flour and blancmange powder together. Add egg and flour alternately to mixture. Beat well ; bake in 2 greased sandwich tins for 20 minutes.

When cold spread with layer of jam. To ice, boil together 2 tablespoonfuls each sugar and water and small piece of margarine. Allow to cool, beat in sufficient pink blancmange powder to make icing of right colour and consistency.—MRS. P. KYLE, Kildare, Burwash, Sussex.

QUEEN CAKES

5 ozs. self-raising flour or 4 ozs. flour and 1 oz. cornflour.
3 ozs. sugar.
2 heaped tablespoonfuls dried egg mixed with 6 tablespoonfuls water.

1½ ozs. margarine.
1½ ozs. lard.
1 oz. raisins or sultanas chopped.
Almond or vanilla flavouring.

Mix dried egg and let it stand while fats and sugar are creamed together. Add egg and flour alternately, sifting latter in, then fruit and a little vanilla or almond flavouring. Beat well, have tin lined with greased paper ready, drop mixture in pieces size of a penny and bake to pale golden brown in hot oven.—L. N. BOND. 2 The Courtway, Carpender's Park, Watford.

ROCK CAKES

⅛ lb. flour.
3 ozs. lard or dripping.
1 teaspoonful baking powder.
Lemon juice or essence to taste (optional).

3 ozs. sultanas.
2 ozs. sugar (brown if possible).
1 reconstituted egg.
Pinch of salt.
Milk to mix.

Rub lard into flour, add other ingredients. Mix all together into dry paste with milk. Break into pieces any size liked and bake in sharp oven 12–15 minutes.

SEED CAKE

⅛ lb. flour.
4 ozs. margarine.
4 ozs. sugar.
2 dried eggs reconstituted and well beaten.
Pinch of mixed spice.

1 teaspoonful baking powder.
1 dessertspoonful carraway or cummin seeds.
1 small teacupful milk.

Beat butter and sugar to a cream. Add eggs. Then flour, baking powder, seeds, spice and milk. Mix all well together. Put at once into greased tin and bake in moderate oven ¾ hour.—MISS HIPWELL. 1 Cambridge Road, Ely, Cambs.

SIMNEL CAKE

7 ozs. self-raising flour.
1 oz. soya flour.
4 ozs. margarine.
3 ozs. sugar.
⅛ lb. dried fruit.
2 level tablespoonfuls dried egg.

1 teaspoonful dried milk.
1 teaspoonful mixed spice.
7 tablespoonfuls water
Marzipan icing (see Fillings).

Sieve flours and mixed spice, rub in fat, add dried fruit and sugar. Whisk dried egg and milk with water, add to dry ingredients, mixing well.

Put half the mixture in greased tin, cover with half the marzipan, put rest of cake mixture on top, bake in moderate oven 1 to 1¼ hours. When cooked, brush ring round top with jam, on this put flat ring of marzipan, leaving circle in centre. Cut paper to fit centre to prevent burning, replace cake in oven till marzipan is golden brown. Take out cake, remove paper, decorate centre with marzipan chicken and eggs. —PEGGIE MACKAY, Elstree.

SPICED FRUIT GINGERBREAD

½ lb. flour.
4 ozs. medium oatmeal.
3 ozs. fat.
3 ozs. sugar.
3 tablespoonfuls golden syrup.
¼ gill prepared household milk.

2 ozs. chopped dates or sultanas.
½ teaspoonful powdered cinnamon.
1 teaspoonful ground ginger.
½ teaspoonful bicarbonate of soda.
Pinch of salt.

Rub fat into flour and oatmeal with a pinch of salt. Put milk and syrup to warm. Add all dry ingredients except fruit to flour and fat. Make a well in centre and pour in warmed syrup and milk. Add fruit. Pour mixture into greased shallow tin and bake 1 hour in a moderately hot oven.—Mrs. P. MacNeill, Paget Road, Stoke Newington, N.16.

SPONGE FINGERS

4 ozs. flour.
4 ozs. sugar.
½ teaspoonful baking powder.

2 ozs. lard and margarine mixed.
2 reconstituted eggs.
A little milk.
¼ teaspoonful salt.

Beat lard and margarine to cream with sugar, beat in egg, then flour, salt, baking powder and enough milk to make slightly runny mixture. Beat until creamy and bake in plain tin, well greased, in moderate oven 15–20 minutes. When cold cut into fingers.—H. M. Addison, Manor Flat, Braunston, Oakham, Rutland.

This is a good basic sponge recipe for cakes or puddings. Flavouring can be added.

WAR-TIME SPONGE

3 ozs. flour.
1 teaspoonful baking powder.
3 ozs. castor sugar.

2 level tablespoonfuls dried egg.
5 tablespoonfuls water.

Put dried egg powder in basin, add 4 tablespoonfuls water, mix thoroughly, then add sugar, beat this well, add flour and baking powder, mix well, leaving no lumps. Then add 1 tablespoonful cold water. This makes the sponge light. Cook in a quick oven, in a shallow round tin, 15–20 minutes. When cold split through centre, spread with jam or flavoured filling.—E. Astley, June Garden, Budleigh Salterton, Devon.

Chapter VII. WHAT to do with CHEESE

A LITTLE cheese can do much in catering. As ingredient in hot vegetable and other savoury dishes, it adds interest and nutritive value. There is also the bowl of grated cheese, which can turn soup, salad or savoury into a complete meal. Home-made oat-cakes or potato cakes are a good accompaniment.

Put bowl of grated cheese on the table for another simple meal—hot potatoes steamed or roasted in their jackets. This addition and plenty of pepper turns jacket potatoes into appetizing savoury.

A QUICK SAVOURY

2 ozs. grated cheese.
1 reconstituted egg.
1 teacupful fine bread-crumbs.

Small teacupful milk, fresh or dried.
Pepper, salt.
Tiny piece of margarine.

Beat up egg, add crumbs, melted margarine, cheese, seasoning and milk. Beat all together. Bake in moderate oven 15 minutes.—N. S., Finchley.

AS A SPREAD

½ lb. cheese, grated.
¾ oz. margarine.
1 teaspoonful salt.

A little less than ¼ pint milk.
1 oz. cornflour or flour to thicken.

Bring milk, margarine and salt to boil in saucepan and thicken with cornflour or flour. Add grated cheese (using up any dry pieces), cook over low heat, stirring all the time till contents of pan become smooth paste. This takes about 8 minutes. While still hot pour soft creamy cheese into jam jar. Suitable for toasts, sandwiches, salad.—MRS. R. C. WILSON, Highwood House, Kingston Hill.

BURMESE RICE

4 ozs. rice.
2 ozs. grated cheese.
3 tomatoes.

1 teaspoonful curry pow-der.
1 oz. margarine.
Salt and pepper.

Boil rice, drain and dry it. Melt margarine in saucepan, put in tomatoes cut into thin slices; shake in curry powder, cook gently 15 minutes. Add rice, cheese and seasoning.

This is an excellent meatless dish but if liked any meat or poultry cut into small pieces can be added. Serve very hot.—MRS. D. Bucknall, 24 Jameson Road, Bexhill-on-Sea.

CHEESE AND TOMATO RISSOLES

4 ozs. grated cheese.	1 oz. fat.
4 ozs. cooked potatoes.	1 teaspoonful sage.
4 ozs. breadcrumbs.	1 teaspoonful flour.
2 tomatoes or equivalent in puree.	Seasoning, dry mustard. Fat for frying.

Put flour, salt, pepper and mustard in basin. Skin tomatoes (this is done easily by scalding them with hot water in basin), pulp them and blend with flour. Put mixture in saucepan, cook three minutes. Stir in the fat, cheese, potatoes, half the breadcrumbs and sage. Put mixture on dish, divide into eight portions, shape into rissoles, dip in flour, roll in remaining breadcrumbs, fry in hot fat. These can be eaten hot, or cold with salad.—MRS. LINDSAY, 2 Paget Road, Stoke Newington, N.16.

CHEESE CROQUETTES—THREE WAYS

(1) *With potato.*

1 cupful mashed potato.	Seasoning.
⅛ to ¼ cupful grated cheese.	A little milk.
1 dried egg (optional).	Breadcrumbs.
Shredded onion.	Frying fat.
Dab of margarine.	

Make potato really smooth with scrap of margarine, season, add shredded onion, dried egg in powder form and cheese. Beat well to make light. If too dry add a little milk. Form into flat thin cakes, coat in breadcrumbs (or brush over with milk) and fry golden brown in hot fat. Serve with salad, hot gravy or salad dressing.

(2) *With macaroni or other paste.*
   Substitute 1 cupful cold cooked macaroni for potato and put through mincer. Add scraps of minced bacon or left-over meat. Proceed as before.

(3) *With cauliflower, cabbage, carrot or swede.*
   Choose a green and a root vegetable. Use two cupfuls, one of each, in place of potato. Proceed as before. Serve with potato chips.

PEA PUREE PANCAKES

1 lb. peas (fresh, dried or tinned).	½ teaspoonful sugar. Dab of margarine.
2 ozs. grated cheese.	Pancakes or fried
1 dessertspoonful chopped mint.	croutons. Seasoning.

Cook peas till tender, adding sugar to water. Drain. Mash peas or rub through sieve, mix in mint, margarine and seasoning. Make two thick pancakes, using one dried or fresh egg (*see* Meatless Dishes). Turn on to hot dish with puree spread between as though for sandwich cake and serve with dish of grated cheese.

Another method is to serve pea puree very hot in bowls with grated cheese and fried croutons made either by cutting up slice of stale bread in small triangles and frying in boiling fat or dipping pieces in gravy and browning on greased tin in oven.—MRS. H. G. GOODALL, The Wardenry, Farley, Salisbury.

PROCESSED CHEESE

Chef of a peace-time luxury liner took charge of one of the great war canteens. He found that tired women war workers ate their bread and salads for supper but left their portions of Cheddar cheese as they could not digest it. This was his brain wave.

Cheese was put through mincer, pressed into small round pots, turned out moulded into baby cheeses, each scored with fork in criss-cross pattern and served on bed of lettuce. There were no more cheese left-overs.—*The Daily Telegraph* HOME COOK.

SECTION II

THE COOKERY of TODAY AND TOMORROW

Chapter I. *ALL-the-YEAR-ROUND SALADS*

THE housewife has new ideas about the salad bowl. It is important in providing quickly prepared and served meals, often fuel-less, that are well balanced. Ingredients come from her own garden or from English farms and nurseries.

Salads are being served with hot as with cold dishes to ensure the necessary fresh food in the diet. They are handed round in addition to hot green or other vegetable. These are the simple salads, crisp lettuce leaves with either radish, tomato, beet or grated carrot, chopped chives or onion.

The salad with fish, cheese or meat may make main meal. When lettuce is not to be had, shredded cabbage or sprouts provide fresh green. The store cupboard helps with pickled pears, cherries and damsons, spiced beetroots, picked walnuts or cabbage. Grated cheese or raw carrot often tops these salads of today.

BEETROOT SALAD

1 or 2 cooked beetroots.	Watercress to garnish.
A little sliced onion.	Seasoning.
Horseradish.	Vinegar.
Chopped parsley.	

Slice beetroots. Put alternate layers in dish, sprinkle with onion and chopped parsley and a very little scraped horseradish. Garnish with watercress. Season with pepper and salt and add a little vinegar, white if possible.

CHERRY SALAD

¾ lb. ripe black cherries
1 lettuce.
Cinnamon or Paprika.

1½ tablespoonfuls of cream dressing (sweet or piquant).

Arrange lettuce, unshredded, in bowl with stoned cherries in centre. Pour dressing over fruit and serve with any cold meat. Excellent with thinly sliced pork or spiced ham. Cheese instead of meat goes well with a piquant dressing. Dust of powdered cinnamon with sweet dressing or paprika with piquant. Strain bottled fruit is suitable using juice as fruit cocktail with tiny leaf of mint and a suggestion of mixed spice.

COLD MEAT MAYONNAISE

4 ozs. diced cold meat.
1 small minced onion.
1 or 2 tomatoes.
Diced cold potato.
¼ cupful diced raw celery or cooked beetroot.

1 lettuce.
Watercress, cucumber or other salading in season.
Chopped parsley or gherkin to garnish.
Home-made mayonnaise.
Seasoning.

Mix diced meat with onion, potato, celery or beetroot, season.

Make a bed of lettuce in salad bowl, pile the meat mixture on it, pour over mayonnaise or salad cream (*see* chapter on Pickles and sauces). Garnish with watercress, or cucumber, parsley or gherkins and sliced tomato.

CUCUMBER SALAD

Cucumber.
Chopped parsley, chervil or chives.

Salad dressing.
Salt.

Prepare this way for *hors d'œuvres* or salad. Cut in cubes or slices. Put in bowl, sprinkling with salt. After 25 minutes drain off moisture. Add plain dressing made without salt. Sprinkle with chervil, parsley or chives.

MOCK CRAB SALAD

3 oz. grated cheese.
1 oz. margarine.
2 teaspoonfuls vinegar.
1 tablespoonful breadcrumbs.

Lettuce.
2 tomatoes.
Seasoning.
Garnish of raw grated carrot.

Line salad bowl with lettuce leaves and arrange sliced tomatoes in outer circle. Beat together all other ingredients, heap in centre. Add garnish. If anchovy sauce is available, sprinkle over 1 teaspoonful. Serve with salad cream.—*The Daily Telegraph* HOME COOK.

PEANUT SALAD

1 tablespoonful peanut butter.	Sliced beetroot or tomato.
	Lettuce.
2 tablespoonfuls mashed potato.	Salad dressing.
	A little grated cheese or chopped ham.
1 teaspoonful chopped onion or 2 teaspoonfuls chives.	Seasoning.

Put peanut butter, potato, onion and seasoning in bowl. Beat well together, form into small balls. Mount each on slice of beetroot or tomato.

Arrange lettuce leaves in bowl and place mounted peanut balls on them. Serve salad dressing separately and a dish of grated cheese or of thinly sliced chopped ham.—*The Daily Telegraph* HOME COOK.

PIQUANT FRUIT SALAD

Lettuce.	Salad cream.
Cold new potatoes.	Cooked green peas or beans.
¼ lb. fresh loganberries, red currants or plums.	Chives or spring onion.
Salt and pepper.	Clove of garlic.
A little sugar.	

Prepare bowl by rubbing round lightly with garlic. Arrange lettuce leaves and sliced new potatoes, with fruit in centre seasoned with salt, pepper and sugar. Add peas, chopped beans and chives. Pour dressing over.—MRS. DALWAY TURNBULL, Grange Mead, Addlestone, Surrey.

RAW VEGETABLE SALAD

2 large carrots.	A little white heart of cabbage.
1 large parsnip.	
2 medium sized turnips.	1 apple (optional).
1 large beetroot.	1 onion (optional).
4 or 5 brussels sprouts.	A little parsley.
1 stick celery.	Clove of garlic (optional).

All ingredients are used raw. Rub bowl with garlic. Mince all ingredients into bowl, leaving in juices. Season well with salt and pepper, mix with home-made mayonnaise or salad cream. Serve. No lettuce needed.

Flavour of this salad is piquant and unusual, with no predominating flavour. The beetroot gives a little sweetening and colour. Celery gives "crunchiness". Salad also makes an excellent *hors d'œuvre.*— E. M., W.8.

RUNNER BEAN SALAD

2 lb. runner beans.	Salt.
Small knob margarine.	Dressing.

Slice beans finely. Melt margarine in saucepan, put in beans. Add a little salt to preserve colour and enough water to prevent burning.

Put lid tightly on saucepan, shake occasionally. Cook 20 minutes. Prepare dressing. Mix well with hot beans and leave to cool. Good with cold meat or fish.

Dressing

ı small onion chopped.
2 tablespoonfuls vinegar.
ı teaspoonful c h o p p e d parsley.

ı teaspoonful sugar.
Pepper and salt to taste.
A little sour milk that has turned thick.

Mix dry ingredients with vinegar and sour milk.

WINTER SALAD

ı2 prunes.
ı½ ozs. grated cheese.
White cabbage heart grated.

2 medium sized raw carrots grated.
Salad cream.

Prepare prunes this way the day before required. They will be delicious. Pour sufficient boiling water over them in small basin to cover. Stand one minute. Pour off. Pour on just enough cold water to cover prunes. Leave 24 hours.

Stone and split prunes almost in half. Stuff with cheese chopped in small pieces, fold halves together. Heap shredded cabbage and carrot on dish. Decorate with stuffed prunes. Serve with salad cream or any home-made dressing.—MISS M. G. WOOD. 27 Brookfield Avenue, Liverpool, 23.

Chapter II. FRUIT in the DAILY MENU

ALL-THE-YEAR-ROUND TABLE JELLY

APPLES and prunes may be used in winter, rhubarb in spring, followed by the soft and stone fruits and later blackberries.

ı lb. fresh fruit.
4 to 6 ozs. sugar

2¼ oz. cornflour or flour (or another ½ oz. if arrowroot is used).

Stew fruit with sugar, rub through sieve. Pulp and juice should measure 1½ pints. Make up with water if short. With a little of this juice, when cold, blend the cornflour to the consistency of cream. Bring the rest of juice to boil. Remove pan from heat, add cornflour, boil for a few minutes, stirring all the time, till it thickens. Pour into wetted mould or individual glasses. When cold turn out. Serve if liked with custard or top of milk. Sufficient for 6 to 8 persons.— MRS. G. DENE, 64 Alumhurst Road, Bournemouth.

If rhubarb is used, flavour to taste with ginger or lemon juice or flavouring. For prune jelly, use ¼ lb. prunes soaked and stewed in 1 pint of water.

APPLE BUTTER

This spread, popular in America, makes a substitute for butter.

Wash and quarter apples without paring or coring; cut out any damaged or maggoty parts. Place in preserving pan with just enough water to cover. Cook slowly till tender. Strain off juice. Rub apples through colander or sieve.

To every pound of pulp allow ½ lb. sugar. Add this to juice, bring to boil, add pulp, cook till mixture is thick and smooth, stirring to prevent burning. Pot in small jars, as when opened it is better used up quickly. Seal while hot.

Any flavouring that suits apple can be added such as the equivalent of 1 orange or 1 lemon to 1 lb. pulp, or vanilla to taste. ¼ teaspoonful cinnamon and a few cloves may also be added; if liked a quince may take place of one or two apples.

BAKED APPLES WITH A DIFFERENCE

Pare large cooking apples, remove cores. Have ready greased dish.

(1) Put a little sugar or treacle and 2 cloves in each hollow, fill with 2 dates.

(2) Bake with a little sugar. Hand round a mixture of ground ginger and sugar.

(3) Put small piece of margarine on plate, mix well with sufficient sugar and pinch of cinnamon. Fill hollow with this.

(4) Fill as in (1) with dates. Serve covered with chocolate or chocolate custard sauce (*see* Sweet Sauces).

In each case add a little water to dish to prevent burning. Baste while cooking.

BLACKCURRANT TART

Bottle of blackcurrants or 1 lb. stewed blackcurrants. Sugar.	½ lb. pastry. 4 ozs. breadcrumbs

Sometimes bottled blackcurrants have tough skins which spoil them for tarts. They can be used this way with success, or fresh fruit may be used.

Press blackcurrants through wire sieve and add sugar to *puree*. Line a deep plate or tin with pastry, half fill with breadcrumbs, add *puree*. Cook as for pastry. Delicious hot or cold.

Any juicy fruit can be used in this way.—Mrs. PAUL AINSWORTH, Five Cross Ways, Cullompton, Devon.

FRESH FRUIT CHARLOTTE

1 lb. raspberries and red-currants or loganberries.	Sugar.
4 ozs. breadcrumbs.	⅛ pint custard made with dried eggs.

Partly fill pie dish with breadcrumbs and fruit. Sprinkle with small quantity of sugar, press all firmly with a fork until crumbs are soaked with juice.

Pour custard over contents of pie dish. Cook till custard has set. When cold decorate with a few fresh raspberries and sprinkle with single redcurrants.—Mrs. T. CROAL, 9 Ember Lane, Esher.

FRESH FRUIT MOULD

Sweetened stewed fruit.	Stale sponge cake or sliced bread.

Prepare any available fruit and cook until tender with half a cupful of water and sugar to taste. Slightly grease a medium sized basin, line it with stale sponge cake or sliced bread. Pour the fruit into the lined basin till well filled, place some sponge or bread slices on top, cover with a plate and a weight. Leave overnight, then turn on to a dish and serve with custard if desired.—Mrs. L. WAYLETT, 38 Waterfall Road, New Southgate, N.11.

FRESH LOGANBERRIES

These are seldom eaten raw, but done in the following way—if the sugar can occasionally be spared—the flavour of this fine fruit can be fully appreciated.

Sprinkle a layer of sugar in a glass bowl or individual glasses, then a layer of loganberries. Continue with alternate layers till bowl or glasses are filled. The last layer must be sugar. Leave for at least 4 hours before serving.

FRUIT FOOL

1 lb. gooseberries, plums, bottled fruit or any soft fruit.	Small tin sweetened condensed milk (if not sweetened add sugar to taste to fruit).
1 gill of water.	

Stew fruit in the water till tender, adding sugar if required. Rub through sieve, leave to cool. Whisk milk in bowl. Add fruit puree gradually, beat well. Pour into individual glasses, serve cold.

Puree and milk mixture if preferred can be stiffened with gelatine (½ oz. to ¼ pint puree). Dissolve gelatine in a little of the juice. Add whisked milk and fruit to it, beat well. Pour into glasses or wetted moulds.—*The Daily Telegraph* HOME COOK.

PARTY WHIP

Apples, soft fruit, cherries or plums can be used for this sweet—the sharper fruits such as plums, currants and loganberries are particularly good. Fresh or bottled fruit may be used.

Sufficient fruit stewed in water to give 1 pint of puree. Sugar to taste.	5 level tablespoonfuls semolina. Little colouring if liked

Stew fruit slowly in water. Strain through sieve, measure off 1 pint of juice. Return this to pan, adding sugar. When almost boiling, sift in semolina slowly, stirring all the time. Boil 3 minutes. Pour into large basin, add puree, whip well with wooden spoon till spoon stands on end or a piece of the whip floats in water. This takes about ¼ hour. Turn into glass dish, serve very cold with mock cream or top of milk.—Mrs. B. GILBERT, 17 The Crescent, Leatherhead.

This is a delicious party sweet, well worth the trouble. A simpler sweet can be made by proceeding as before up to the point where the puree semolina is boiled for 3 minutes. Then instead of whipping, cook gently another 10–15 minutes, using if possible a double saucepan

TO KEEP FRUIT FRESH

Any soft fruit, particularly currants and raspberries, can be treated in this way.

1 lb. any soft fruit. 1 dessertspoonful gelatine.	¼ cupful water. Sufficient sugar to sweeten.

Stalk or otherwise prepare fruit, place in serving bowl or individual glasses. Place water with sugar in pan over heat, dissolve gelatine in it. Add sweetened gelatine to fruit, allow to set. This will preserve uncooked fruit in its first freshness and will keep well for a few days.

Remnants of jam pot can be used to sweeten in place of sugar and are clarified by gelatine. Colouring may be added for red fruits.—MISS J. A. STEVENS, Medway, Fordcombe, Kent.

Chapter III. CANNED FOODS, POWDERED MILK and EGGS

THE ready-to-hand store foods which give the housewife a sense of security against unexpected calls on catering have extended their already wide range to include dried eggs and milk as well as canned fare. The store cupboard with these highly important additions can always provide a quick meal for family or unexpected guest.

Especially appreciated nowadays are the fuel-saving virtues of canned meats, fish and vegetables. Simple additions and little or no cooking turn them into satisfying, appetising dishes.

If canned meat, fish and fruit are said to encourage "the housewife who cooks with the tin opener", dried eggs and milk, by rousing her interest in new methods, have helped to raise cookery standards.

A PARTY SWEET

1 small can of any fruit.	2 dessertspoonfuls (½ oz.) gelatine.
1 heaped dessertspoon-ful flour.	

Drain liquid in can from fruit, make it up with water to 2 breakfast-cupfuls (about 1 pint). Mix flour to smooth paste with a little of the liquid, bring remainder of liquid to boil, stir in flour, boil 2 minutes till thick. Pour on to gelatine, stirring. Cool, whisk at least 15 minutes. Chop up fruit and add. Pour into serving dish, leave to set. Enough for 6 people.

This sweet looks and tastes as though it had both cream and white of egg in it. The longer it is whisked, the lighter and creamier it will be. Can also be made with juice from stewed fruit, with no fruit added or with black coffee.—MRS. J. B. LOWE, The Sheiling, Box Wiltshire.

BEANS AND GREENS

Can of beans.	Cooked cabbage, sprouts or spinach.
Dried herbs.	
Fat to fry.	White sauce or tomato sauce.

Strain tin of beans free of brine. Dry and brown in a little boiling fat in frying pan. Sprinkle with dried herbs, serve on bed of chopped cabbage, spinach or sprouts dressed with white sauce or tomato sauce.

BEANS AU GRATIN

Can of beans.	Browned breadcrumbs.
Cheese sauce.	Dabs of margarine.

Strain beans as before. Put in fireproof dish, cover with cheese sauce, sprinkle with breadcrumbs and dabs of margarine, brown

under grill. Serve with young greens, savoy or runner beans.
Beans served with fried sausages and tomatoes make a main dish.
—*The Daily Telegraph* HOME COOK.

PILCHARD OR HERRING CROQUETTES

1 can pilchards or her-
rings.
¼ lb. mashed potato.
1 tablespoonful chopped
parsley.
1 small teaspoonful an-
chovy sauce.

1 oz. margarine.
1 dessertspoonful dried
egg, reconstituted.
Pepper and salt.
A little flour.
Browned breadcrumbs.

Remove bones and skin from fish, flake finely. Sieve potatoes. Melt
margarine in saucepan, add to it the fish, potatoes, parsley, anchovy
sauce, seasoning and egg. Mix thoroughly over heat. Leave to
cool. Flour hands, form into croquettes, and roll in toasted breadcrumbs. Fry golden brown.

QUICK FRUIT DUMPLINGS

Large tin cherries or
other fruit.
2 cupfuls flour.
3 teaspoonfuls baking powder.

¼ teaspoonful salt.
1 tablespoonful sugar.
1 cupful milk.
2 tablespoonfuls fat.

Rub fat into flour and other dry ingredients, make into very soft
dough with milk. Bring fruit with juice to boil in pan, using one that
has tight lid. When boiling drop dumpling mixture by tablespoonfuls
on to fruit. Cover at once very tightly, cook without raising lid for
15 minutes. Serve hot.—MRS. E. AIREY, 5 Newborough Avenue,
Liverpool.

SALMON MOUSSE

1 large tin salmon (Grade
3 is suitable).
2 large slices of bread,
one-inch thick.
1 reconstituted egg.
1 tablespoonful vinegar.

1 teaspoonful finely chopped chives or spring
onion.
1 dessertspoonful parsley
or chervil.

Remove bones and skin of salmon. Put in basin and beat well.
Cut crusts from bread, soak in water, squeeze gently with palms of
hands, mix with salmon. Add plenty of seasoning and the herbs.
Mix all with vinegar (tarragon if possible) and egg. Grease basin, fill
with mixture. Cover with paper or cloth, steam 1¼ hours. Serve hot
or cold.

*　　　*　　　*　　　*　　　*

DRIED EGGS IN MODERN COOKERY

WOMEN are taking kindly to new ways of cookery. Powdered eggs, regarded critically when first put on the market as a substitute for the shell eggs in short supply, now have their own and it may be an enduring place in good home cookery. Dried egg cult is a fascinating and progressive branch of present-day catering.

To reconstitute or not is often the question when preparing dishes. Here is the answer:

In cakes, puddings and other dishes in which dry ingredients are mixed together and then made into a dough or stiff batter, neither dried egg nor dried milk need be mixed with water beforehand. If preferred they may be blended in with the dry ingredients before any liquid is added.

Experience has convinced many housewives that this method of sieving in egg and milk powder with dry ingredients makes lighter puddings and cakes which rise better, besides being quicker and saving washing up.

When dried egg is reconstituted, the secret is to mix it very smoothly, taking time to remove all lumps. A pinch of bicarbonate of soda or baking powder is sometimes added when mixing. Lumps disappear quickly and resultant mixture is very smooth. Some women prefer to mix with milk. Food experts disagree with this opinion and recommend mixing with water only. Home cooks pursue the method they have found most successful, whether with or without water.

DRIED EGGS HARD BOILED

Reconstitute dried egg, beating well. Add seasoning and if liked a little chopped chives and parsley. Grease a cup, fill with mixture, put it covered into pan of boiling water and steam for about 10 minutes. Use this "hard-boiled" egg chopped as a garnish.

To use in Scotch eggs, put in an egg cup instead of a cup. See that water does not get in.—R. C., Parkgate.

ROOSEVELT SCRAMBLE

Scrambled or buttered eggs are President Roosevelt's favourite food. "And he likes them so well," Mrs. Roosevelt has said, "that I believe he would eat them at every meal if I would serve them to him."

No less an authority on epicurean cookery than the late M. Escoffier went so far as to declare that scrambled eggs were the finest of all egg dishes—always provided the eggs were not overcooked.

*   *   *   *   *

Reconstitute dried egg with water or milk and water. Add grated cheese if liked, or onion, chopped chives, tomato or parsley, minced cold fried bacon or cold meat or cold vegetables.

Into fairly thick bottomed pan with tight fitting lid put a knob of margarine and 1 tablespoonful tepid water. Pour in mixture, put lid on tight, set over slow jet, leave about 10 minutes. Do not stir. When centre of upper surface is creamily set but actually cooking, serve. This may be turned into a sweet and served with hot jam.— F. A. K., Greywell.

TO MAKE OMELET WITH DRIED EGG

First method

1 tablespoonful dried egg each person.	Seasoning.
Water.	Lard for cooking.

Mix dried egg very smoothly, using the proper proportion of water —two tablespoonfuls to each tablespoonful dried egg. Season, beat well. Stand half an hour. Just before pouring into pan add one small tablespoonful more water and whisk again.

Lard is best for cooking. When pan is smoking hot, pour mixture in quickly and keep shaking the pan slightly, stirring the mixture very lightly with a fork. When beginning to thicken, loosen round edge with palette knife. Tilt pan, still stirring, so that the liquid part runs round edges and underneath. Keep shaking the pan slightly. When bottom is brown and top not quite set, fold over, turn omelet on to hot plate and serve.

Some people, after folding the omelet over, place it in pan under the grill for a few seconds. This makes it fluff up.

Second method

An omelet in which the dried egg is mixed partly with milk appeals to some.

4 level tablespoonfuls dried egg.	5 tablespoonfuls milk.
4 tablespoonfuls water.	Seasoning.

Mix dried egg with water, mixing well till very smooth. Then add milk, mix well and beat. Season, leave at least 15 minutes. Beat mixture slightly just before pouring quickly into hot fat in pan. Cook as before.—A. D., N.W.3.

BACON OMELET

Save bacon fat for several days. Fry a small rasher of bacon, remove from pan, chop up. Put saved bacon fat in pan. Mix dried eggs as directed, using equivalent of one shell egg per person, add 1 dessertspoonful milk, seasoning. Make omelet in bacon fat. When nearly ready add chopped bacon, fold over and serve immediately on hot plates. Grated cheese can be used instead of bacon.

Be careful not to let omelet catch. Dried eggs do so more easily than shell eggs.—E. H., W.14.

*   *   *   *

HOW DRIED MILK CAN HELP

MANY little treats can be provided with the help of a tin of dried milk. It represents two important ingredients—the powder and the reconstituted milk. Housewives are not yet at the end of experimenting with the powder which professional cooks have long used in a great variety of ways. Its "stickiness" and the fact that it blends well with sweet flavourings are useful in the making of sweetmeats. It also provides an excellent mock cream or cake filling and good salad cream (*see* these sections). In the form of liquid milk, it is invaluable in the making of meatless dishes and puddings.

TO MIX POWDERED MILK

The use of an egg whisk is a simpler, quicker method than that advised on the tin. After putting lukewarm water in wide-necked jug, whisk thoroughly. With an egg whisk no lumps are formed, but these are difficult to avoid if a fork is used. Whisked milk will not burn so easily.

*   *   *   *

Instead of warm water, mix dried milk with the same quantity of lukewarm coffee. This makes delicious boiled custard, using custard powder. Rice, sago, semolina and queen pudding are also delicious made with the "coffee milk" instead of with plain milk.

Made rather thick, whipped with an egg whisk and put in the refrigerator, "coffee milk" resembles a cold souffle or is a good filling for flan.

"Coffee milk" may also be used to mix cakes and is recommended in a chocolate cake.—MRS. R. S. WALFORD, 8 Molyneux Court, Tunbridge Wells.

YORKSHIRE PUDDING

4 ozs. plain flour.	Pinch of salt.
1 tablespoonful dried egg.	Lard or cooking fat.
2½ l e v e l tablespoonfuls milk powder and ½ pint water or ½ pint milk.	

Sieve together flour, dried egg, milk powder and salt. Press out all lumps. Gradually beat in cold water (or fresh milk, omitting milk powder) to make thin batter. Stand ½ hour. Give batter another good beating and then pour into tin or small tins in which fat is smoking hot.

Another Method

2 heaped tablespoonfuls flour.	Pinch of salt.
1 fresh or reconstituted egg.	½ pint fresh or household milk.

Beat flour, salt and milk together with wooden spoon. Add whisked egg and beat again. Allow to stand, pour into tin as before.

LIQUID CANNED MILK

This is invaluable in the making of sweets, cake fillings and as mock cream to serve with fruit. It is important to remember that this milk, whether or not full cream standard, has a concentrated flavour.

Simple "snow" type sweets with a party air are created by whipping up this milk with gelatine and fruit juice, coffee or chocolate flavouring.

CAKE FILLING OR MOCK CREAM

First method

With gelatine. (*See* chapter on Sauces).

Second method

Some people prefer canned milk whipped up without gelatine. Full-cream milk is best. Milk has first to be heated in order that colloidal or fatty substances may thicken but must get really cold (though not frozen) before whipping.

Put can in cold water. It is not necessary to pierce top, as milk does not get really hot. Bring water to boil, boil 2–5 minutes.

Chill can of milk in refrigerator or in cold water in cold place Leave till really cold (1 or 2 hours in case of refrigerator). Whip thoroughly with, if liked, a little sugar, till it resembles whipped cream.

Chapter IV. OATMEAL HELPS HOME COOKS

BACON OATMEAL PUDDING

2 teacupfuls medium oatmeal.	2 small chopped onions or leeks.
3 ozs. chopped suet or dripping.	Seasoning to taste. Water.
2 rashers fat bacon.	

Line bottom of greased basin with chopped bacon. Mix other ingredients ; add water to make a fairly stiff dough. Pour mixture over the chopped bacon. Cover with cloth and boil 3 hours. Serve with gravy and green vegetable.

Any remaining pudding can be sliced and fried for breakfast.

DERBYSHIRE OATCAKES

1 lb. fine oatmeal.	Pinch of salt.
Smal teacupful flour.	¼ teaspoonful sugar.
½ oz. yeast.	Frying fat.
Teacupful tepid water.	

Cream yeast with sugar and add about a teacupful of tepid water. When it begins to ferment, add it to mixed oatmeal, flour and salt, and make into thin batter with cold water.

Leave overnight, stir well and when required cook in frying pan like pancakes. These oatcakes are good either fried in bacon fat or toasted and spread with dripping. Also excellent, well toasted, to eat with cheese.—M. D., Buxton.

MOCK HARE SOUP

2 large potatoes.	2 cloves.
1 leek.	1½ pints stock or water.
1 carrot.	½ oz. dripping.
1 stick celery.	Pepper and salt to taste.
½ turnip.	1 teaspoonful meat es-
5 ozs. coarse oatmeal.	sence or cube.

Chop vegetables, put in pan with dripping and fry thoroughly. Add oatmeal and cook until brown, stirring all the time to prevent burning. Add seasoning, cloves, and stock and cook ½ hour on low heat. Sieve before serving, add meat essence and re-heat.—G. A. BARCLAY, Sundial House, Park Hill Road, Torquay.

OATMEAL CAKE

½ lb. fine oatmeal.	½ teaspoonful cream of
4 ozs. sugar.	tartar.
4 ozs. dried fruit.	1 reconstituted egg.
4 ozs. margarine.	Little grated nutmeg.
1 teaspoonful bicarbon-	About ¼ pint fresh or
ate of soda.	household milk.
	Pinch of salt.

Grease and flour a Yorkshire pudding tin. Sieve the flour, salt, bicarbonate of soda, cream of tartar and nutmeg into a basin. Rub in the fat with the tips of the fingers until mixture resembles fine breadcrumbs, then add the sugar and fruit and mix well. Stir in the egg beaten up well in the milk to form a fairly soft mixture.

Bake in a hot oven until golden brown, then slightly lower heat and bake until firm. When cold cut into fingers.—MRS. W. S. FLETCHER, Wellow Cottage, Nr. Newark, Notts.

OATMEAL AND WHOLEMEAL BREAD

½ lb. wholemeal flour.	1 teaspoonful bicarbon-
6 ozs. medium or coarse	ate of soda.
oatmeal.	1 teaspoonful salt.
2 teaspoonfuls cream of	Milk and water to mix.
tartar (not required if	
sour milk is used).	

Mix dry ingredients. Add enough milk and water to make stiff dough. Work together as quickly as possible with hands and put in floured tin or form into round loaf. Bake in fairly hot oven for about 40 minutes.—LADY JANET GORE, Fyning Combe, Rogate, Petersfield.

VEGETABLE AND OATMEAL GOULASH

1 lb. mixed root vegetables.	1 teaspoonful meat essence or cube.
2 ozs. coarse or medium oatmeal.	Sprinkling of paprika.
Knob of dripping.	Chopped parsley and herbs to flavour.
Vegetable stock.	Pepper and salt to taste.

Prepare and dice vegetables. Fry in dripping until slightly cooked; add oatmeal and stir over fire until fat is absorbed. Season with herbs, pepper and salt and add meat extract. Cover with vegetable stock and simmer gently for 1 hour.

A little corned beef, cooked meat or fish may be added last thing.— MRS. E. M. HOLLOWAY, Harewood Park, Hereford.

Chapter V. THE NEW PASTRY MAKING

GOOD well-baked pastry is a splendid help in making meat or fruit go a long way. Home cooks, combining their own practical experience and official advice, have worked out recipes which are suitable for use with national flour.

Sometimes the flour ingredient is varied by the addition of other meals or potatoes and this again demands a new technique in pastry-making.

SHORT CRUST

½ lb. flour.	½ teaspoonful baking powder.
2 ozs. cooking fat.	

Sieve flour with baking powder. Put fat into the middle of the flour, cut it quickly with a knife. Rub fat into flour as finely as possible, till mixture is almost like breadcrumbs. Follow the Golden Rule of pastry making and use as little cold water as possible, keeping the dough as dry as you can, smooth but stiff. Knead lightly till it leaves sides of the bowl quite clean. Roll out. *Officially recommended.*

If pastry is for a sweet pie or tart, a teaspoonful of sugar added with baking powder to flour improves flavour. If for meat pie, a saltspoonful of salt may be added. National flour is better for a little extra seasoning.

POTATO SHORT CRUST

½ lb. national flour.
4 ozs. sieved cooked potato.
3 ozs. fat.

2 teaspoonfuls baking powder.
½ teaspoonful salt.
Water.

Sieve flour, baking powder and salt. Rub in fat. Add potato and mix to a dry dough with water. Knead.—Miss R. M. ANDERSON, 17 Admiralty Road, Felpham, Bognor Regis.

PASTRY FOR FRESH FRUIT SHORTCAKE

½ lb. self-raising flour.
4 ozs. margarine.
2 ozs. castor sugar.
1 prepared dried egg.

½ teaspoonful baking powder.
Pinch of salt.
A little milk to mix.

Cream warmed fat and sugar. Add egg and a little flour. Mix well. Gradually sift in rest of flour to which salt has been added, using milk to make soft dough.

Divide in two, put into greased sandwich tins. Bake 25–30 minutes.

Spread one round with sweetened crushed fresh fruit or stewed apple puree. Cover with other layer. Sprinkle with sugar.—*The Daily Telegraph* HOME COOK.

RAISED PIE CRUST

6 ozs. flour.
2½ ozs. lard.
2 tablespoonfuls boiling water.

1 saltspoonful salt.
1 gill stock or water.
1 teaspoonful gelatine.

Melt lard in boiling water, bring just to boil. Sieve flour and salt into basin. Make well in centre, pour in fat and water, stirring in flour with knife. Dough should be as dry as possible but if required a little more boiling water may be added. Mix quickly with fingers, knead into one lump, roll out and cut two rounds to fit tin top and bottom and a long piece for sides. Line warmed greased tin. Pack in chopped seasoned meat, put on round of pastry, seeing that edges are pressed together closely. A double edge may be put round top. Decorate top a little and make hole in centre.

Bake in moderate oven 1½ hours if meat is raw, half that time for cooked meat.

When pie is removed from oven, pour in melted jelly through hole in top. Use any jelly from meat (if available) and make it up to a gill by adding warm water in which 1 teaspoonful of gelatine is dissolved. Or use 1 gill of stock or hot water in which a little meat essence is dissolved, adding gelatine as before.

SUET PASTRY

Any left-overs from suet crust make a useful pastry. Make crust in the usual way, but if packet suet is not used, grate suet as finely as possible.

Crust should be rolled wafer thin and can then be used instead of short crust for tartlets, Eccles cakes or baked jam roll. Brush top of pastry with a little re-constituted egg or milk and sprinkle with sugar before baking in oven in same way as ordinary pastry.

WHOLEMEAL FLOUR ROUGH PUFF

½ lb. wholemeal flour.
4 ozs. lard.
½ teacupful water.

1 teaspoonful baking powder.

Put flour in basin, adding baking powder. With palette or cooking knife chop in the lard. When pieces of fat are the size of a nut, make well in centre and add water gradually, all the time chopping the mixture, till it is moderately stiff. With the knife fold over the dough towards you and roll. Do this three times and roll out to size required. Do not handle at all.—Mrs. A. R. WILLIAMS, Woodfield, Malthouse Lane, Kenilworth.

SECTION III

SNACK SERVICE

SNACK fare, savoury and sweet, meets any-hour demand on larder and store. Snack fare is labour and fuel saving. Trolley laid with colourful tray cloths simplifies preparations for the meal and saves laundry. Gaily painted washable tray that can appear uncovered is useful for the late-comer's meal.

Soup cups and individual bowls and glasses save space on trolley or tray. Food too economises in labour and fuel. Finger foods can be satisfying if well thought out and many snacks are suitable for more formal meals of the day.

Today sandwiches, hot and cold, are more than ever in request. Fillings have changed ; housewives are exercising much ingenuity in working out new spreads for sandwiches and hot toasts that make satisfying portable or impromptu home meal.

Toasts are among the quickest ways of answering the call for a hot emergency or odd hour meal.

Individualism in sweets is true kitchen economy as opposed to the communal bowl or mould. Small glasses, darioles, decorative china basins, little fireproof earthenware or glass dishes not only look inviting but give the cook opportunity to use up oddments.

Chapter I. THE SAVOURY SNACK

CELERY WELSH RAREBIT

4 sticks celery.	1 tablespoonful d r i e d milk.
A little grated cheese.	
¼ gill celery stock.	¼ teaspoonful made mustard.

Boil celery till tender in slightly salted water. Put on fireproof dish. Take celery stock, stir in cheese, mustard and dried milk. Cook slowly till cheese is melted, then pour over celery. Brown under grill. Garnish with triangles of toast and parsley.—MRS. A. WHITTICK, 27 Prince Road, S.E. 25.

CHEESE ROLLS

Short or potato pastry (*see* Pastry). Margarine.	Cheese. Seasoning. Cayenne.

Roll out potato pastry, cut into strips 6 inches long by 4 inches wide. In centre place a thin strip of margarine and on top an oblong of cheese half an inch in thickness. Seasoning and cayenne to taste. Roll, pressing edges firmly together. Place on greased tin and bake in fairly hot oven.—H. W., Witheridge.

EGG MAYONNAISE SANDWICHES

Fresh or dried eggs. Margarine.	Mayonnaise sauce. Thin slices of bread.

Prepare buttered eggs with sufficient fresh or reconstituted dried eggs. Set aside to cool.

To make Mayonnaise Sauce

Unsweetened canned milk. 4 teaspoonfuls sugar. ¼ teaspoonful salt.	¼ teaspoonful dry mustard. Vinegar. Cayenne pepper.

Mix mustard with little vinegar into a paste, add salt and sugar, milk to make required quantity, then vinegar drop by drop, stirring well, until desired thickness is obtained. Add a dash of cayenne pepper, add all to buttered egg. Make into sandwiches in usual way.—E. CUREN, Adelphi, Strand.

HADDOCK TOAST

½ small haddock or other smoked fish. ½ oz. margarine. ½ oz. flour. ¼ pint milk. 1 egg, reconstituted.	1 teaspoonful chopped parsley. Dash of anchovy sauce. Pepper, salt. Cayenne. Slices of toast.

Cook haddock, remove skin and bones. Flake it. Melt margarine in saucepan, stir in flour, mix in milk stirring till smooth. Cook a few minutes. Add anchovy essence, parsley, salt, pepper and fish. Stir till thoroughly hot. Add beaten egg, cook a minute or two but do not let it boil. Spread on hot toast, sprinkle with cayenne and put under grill to get light golden brown.

HOT CHEESE SANDWICH

3 ozs. grated cheese.	Seasoning.
1 tablespoonful chutney.	1 teaspoonful vinegar.
2 ozs. dripping or margarine.	Slices of bread.
	Fat for frying.

Beat dripping or margarine to a cream, add grated cheese, chutney, seasoning and vinegar. Spread thickly between slices of bread, fry in hot fat till golden brown and hot through.—F. H., Southsea.

HOT MEAT SANDWICHES

Cooked canned meat	Brown or tomato sauce
Margarine.	Fat for frying.
Slices of bread.	

Spread bread thinly with margarine, arrange meat on slice, cover with another slice of bread and margarine. Tie sandwiches with white thread. Make fat hot in pan, fry sandwiches on both sides.

Have ready thick brown gravy or ordinary white sauce flavoured with tomato. Remove cotton from sandwiches, pour sauce over just before serving. This dish must be kept very hot and the sandwiches crisp.

KENTISH PASTIES

These pasties are most popular at the Pie Stations in Sevenoaks Rural District and can be served hot, or cold make excellent snacks or packed lunches.

Filling

¼ lb. boiled rice.	2 ozs. raw grated carrot.
4 ozs. grated cheese.	Pepper and salt.

Mix these ingredients well.

Pastry

¾ lb. flour.	Pinch of salt.
3 ozs. cooking fat.	Water to mix.

Place a heaped tablespoonful of cheese mixture on centre of a round of pastry. Damp edges and fold as for Cornish pasties. Bake in hot oven ½ hour.—G. M. WARNER, School House, Brasted.

PIQUANT SANDWICH FILLING

1½ ozs. processed cheese (see Cheese section).	½ teaspoonful newly made mustard.
1 dessertspoonful finely chopped watercress.	

Beat together all ingredients well. This makes a sandwich filling with a kick.

SARDINE SAVOURIES

Croutes

Sardines.   Anchovy paste.
Slices of bread.   Curry powder.
Fat for frying.

Put fat in pan. Fry bread in boiling fat, remove from pan. Have ready sardines mashed with anchovy paste and a little curry powder. Spread fried bread first with anchovy paste, then with sardine mixture. Serve hot or cold.—E. CUREN, Adelphi, Strand, W.C.2.

Filling

3 boned sardines.   ½ oz. margarine.
1 tablespoonful l i g h t l y   Pepper.
   scrambled dried egg *or* 1   Dash of vinegar (white
   tablespoonful mashed   preferable).
   potato.   Paprika (optional).

Mix together all ingredients, making mixture very smooth.—*The Daily Telegraph* HOME COOK.

Variations

Tarragon vinegar instead   Instead of vinegar use 1
   of white vinegar.   teaspoonful   tomato
¼ teaspoonful finely chop-   sauce or dash of Wor-
   ped chives.   cester sauce or lemon
                                      substitute.

Fried Sandwiches

A few sardines.   Grated cheese.
Strips of hot fried bread.   Anchovy sauce.

Bone sardines, place them on the fried bread with a little grated cheese. Place another strip of hot fried bread on top, then a little anchovy sauce. Put in hot oven a few minutes and serve hot.—G. D., W.8.

Rolls

Sardines.   Pastry.
Pepper.   ½ reconstituted egg.
Dash of vinegar or lemon   Fat for frying.
   substitute.

Halve and bone required number of sardines. Season with pepper and dash of vinegar. Place on squares of thinly rolled out pastry, fold over, brush with well-beaten egg. Fry golden brown in hot fat or bake in oven.—*The Daily Telegraph* HOME COOK.

*   *   *   *   *

SAVOURY TARTLETS

Line small patty tins with short pastry rolled out thinly and use one of the following fillings :

Curried Egg.—Reconstituted egg scrambled with a little curry paste.

Fish.—Any cooked left-overs, smoked haddock, fresh cod, etc., are suitable. Flake fish finely, mix with very little thick white sauce and a dash of anchovy sauce.

Kipper.—Fill with kipper paste made by mashing kipper with margarine, milk and pepper.

Mushroom.—Fried mushrooms chopped finely, a little thick white sauce to bind, chopped parsley added and sprinkled sparingly with cayenne.

SPICED PRUNE AND BACON ROLLS

¼ lb. prunes.	Cloves.
A little vinegar	Fried squares of bread.
Bacon rashers.	Parsley.

Wash prunes, pour on boiling water to cover. Soak overnight, drain and stone. Dip prunes in a little vinegar. Drain again. Roll a rasher of bacon round two or three prunes, fasten with a clove. Grill or fry the rolls and serve hot on fried squares of bread. Top with a sprig of parsley.

A good snack dish or appetising for lunch served with brussels sprouts and mashed potatoes.—MRS. M. E. YOUNG, Bletchington Park, Bletchington, Oxon.

STUFFED FRESH TOMATOES

Thick squares of bread spread with margarine.	Few chopped shrimps or prawns.
One tomato for each person.	Pepper, salt.
Chopped parsley.	Home-made mayonnaise.

Cut off top from each tomato. Remove some of the pulp, put into bowl with chopped shrimps, season, mix thoroughly with mayonnaise.

Fill tomatoes with mixture, sprinkle with a little finely chopped parsley and mount on bread and butter square.

TOAST CROQUE MONSIEUR

Here is an adapted form of the dish known to chefs as Croque Monsieur.

Thin slices of Spam or similar meat.
1 breakfastcupful thick white sauce.
1 tablespoonful dried egg.

3 tablespoonfuls grated cheese.
Seasoning.
Toast.

Stir dried egg and grated cheese into white sauce. Season and stir well. Put Spam or other meat on each slice of freshly made toast, cover with cheese mixture, brown under grill or in hot oven.—MRS LANGLEY Mill House, Wilsford, Marlborough.

TOMATO FILLING

Excellent for carried lunches or teatime sandwiches.

½ lb. tomatoes.
2 ozs. grated cheese
2 ozs. breadcrumbs.
2 ozs. margarine.

1 dried or fresh egg.
1 small onion.
Salt and pepper.

Scald tomatoes in very hot water for a few minutes, when they will peel easily. Beat up with a fork. Melt margarine, pour over well-beaten egg, add cheese, breadcrumbs, seasoning. Mix with tomatoes. Chop up onion finely and add. Put mixture in saucepan, bring to boil but do not let it boil. Mix well. Put in basin and use when cold. —NESTA GORE. 55 Wesley Park Road, Selly Oak, Birmingham 29.

Chapter II. THE BISCUIT TIN

AFTERNOON CHOCOLATE BISCUITS

1½ ozs. margarine.
2 ozs. flour and 1½ ozs. cornflour or 3½ ozs. flour.

¾ oz. cocoa.
1½ ozs. sugar.
1 teaspoonful dried egg.
1 tablespoonful milk.

Cream margarine and sugar. Work flours and cocoa into creamed mixture and add dried egg mixed with the milk. Do not use any more liquid, but work mixture with your hand. Roll out very thinly on floured board. Cut into small rounds with fluted cutter. Bake in moderate over 12 minutes.

Put two rounds together with "butter" icing made of equal parts margarine and sugar flavoured with essence or cocoa. Jam can be used instead.—O. M., Huntingdon.

ALMOND BISCUITS

⅛ lb. flour.
1 dried egg, (reconstituted).
1 small teaspoonful baking powder.

4 ozs. margarine.
2½ ozs. sugar.
½ teaspoonful almond essence.

Rub fat into flour and add remaining ingredients. Roll out, cut into strips and bake in moderate oven. Biscuits should be a delicate pale brown.—*The Daily Telegraph* HOME COOK.

BRANDY SNAPS

¼ lb. flour.
2 tablespoonfuls syrup.
3 ozs. margarine.

1½ tablespoonfuls sugar.
1 teaspoonful ground ginger.

Melt together syrup, margarine and sugar. Add flour and ground ginger. Mix well and drop in small spoonfuls on well-greased oven sheet. Bake in moderate oven 10 minutes. Biscuits should be a rich brown. Remove from tin with knife and roll up quickly while still warm. May be filled with mock cream or stiff custard.—THE HOME COOK.

CRUNCHIES

5 ozs. plain flour.
4 ozs. medium oatmeal.
2 ozs. sugar.
1 teaspoonful baking powder.

4 ozs. margarine, lard or clarified dripping.
2 ozs. syrup.
Vanilla flavouring.

Cream together the fat, sugar and syrup. Add flour, oatmeal, baking powder and a few drops of vanilla. Knead until the mixture binds. Roll out about ¼ inch thick, cut into rounds or fingers. Bake in moderate oven till golden brown for about 20 minutes. These biscuits keep well stored in air-tight tins.—L. M. SETH-SMITH, Tangle Oak, Telbridge, East Grinstead.

DIGESTIVE BISCUITS

6 ozs. wholemeal flour.
1 oz. plain flour.
1 oz. medium oatmeal.
3 ozs. fat.
1 tablespoonful sugar.
¼ teaspoonful salt.

¼ teaspoonful bicarbonate of soda.
1 teaspoonful cream of tartar.
⅛ teacupful warm milk.

Mix all dry ingredients together, rub in fat and use warm milk to make a stiff dough. Knead and roll out. Cut into rounds, prick with fork. Bake about 10 minutes in moderate oven.—MRS. BURDGE, Chestnut Farm, Yatton, Bristol.

DINNER BISCUITS

To serve with stewed fruit or with chocolate or coffee flavoured sweet.

4 ozs. flour.
1 oz. sugar.
2½ ozs. margarine.

Few drops of vanilla, orange or lemon essence.

Mix well into paste—no liquid required. Roll out to ½ inch thickness. Cut into fingers. Bake quickly until pale golden brown.

Makes nice sandwich biscuit with jam spread between two biscuits.

FLAPJACKS

½ lb. rolled oats.
1 saltspoonful salt.
4 ozs. margarine.

2 ozs. sugar.
2½ tablespoonfuls golden syrup.

Put oats and salt in bowl. Melt margarine, syrup and sugar in saucepan and pour over oats. Mix well with wooden spoon. Grease shallow tin, put mixture in, pressing well down and into corners. Bake in moderate oven 30–45 minutes until crisp and light brown. When cool cut in oblongs 5 inches long by 2 inches wide. Store in tin when cold.—MISS D. GEAREY, Boys' School House, Berkhamsted.

If stickier flapjacks are liked, use a smaller quantity of rolled oats, from 4–6 ozs.

GINGER BISCUITS

6 ozs. flour.
1 tablespoonful sugar and
2 tablespoonfuls golden syrup *or* all in sugar.

3 ozs. margarine.
1 teaspoonful ground ginger.
A little milk if needed.

Warm margarine and treacle over low heat, add dry ingredients and mix well. Use a little milk if necessary but dough should be stiff. Knead till flour is absorbed, roll out thinly, cut into fingers or rounds. Bake 10–15 minutes in hot oven.—*The Daily Telegraph* HOME COOK.

MACAROONS

2½ ozs. sugar.
2 ozs. medium oatmeal.
1 dessertspoonful semolina.

½ oz. margarine.
½ teaspoonful almond essence.
½ reconstituted egg.

Mix sugar, oatmeal and semolina together. Beat in egg and add melted margarine and almond essence. Beat for five minutes, drop on tin, leaving space for spreading, and bake in moderate oven for 10 minutes.—MRS. G. BOWYER, 8 Milton Road, Cambridge.

Another Method

4 ozs. flour.	4 ozs. rolled oats.
3 ozs. lard or lard and margarine.	1½ tablespoonfuls golden syrup.
1 teaspoonful baking powder.	1 tablespoonful sugar.
	Almond essence.

Beat golden syrup, fat and almond essence together. Mix together dry ingredients and then beat into fat mixture. Drop on greased baking sheet; bake 20 minutes.—K. M. G., Merioneth.

PLAIN BISCUITS

6 ozs. flour.	1 oz. margarine.
½ teaspoonful baking powder.	Saltspoonful salt.
	Tepid water.

Well blend margarine with flour, add salt and baking powder. Mix into smooth stiff dough with tepid water. Beat dough well with rolling pin on floured board. Roll out thinly. Fold into three, beat well again; repeat this three times. Roll out very thinly, prick well with fork, cut in rounds or squares and bake in quick oven until done (7–10 minutes).—M. H., London, E.4.

TEA-TIME BISCUITS

8 ozs. flour.	3 ozs. sugar.
3 ozs. margarine.	1 tablespoonful fruit.
1 dried egg, reconstituted.	½ teaspoonful mixed spice.

Rub fat into flour with other dry ingredients, adding prepared egg and if necessary a little milk; but mixture must be stiff enough to roll out thinly. Cut into rounds and bake in moderate oven 10–15 minutes. Fruit may be omitted and biscuit flavoured with small teaspoonful ground ginger or cinnamon or with almond essence.

Chapter III. BEVERAGES IN VARIETY:

SOUPS, CUPS and CORDIALS

HOT nightcaps for cold nights, refreshing home-made summer cups, mulled fruit wines that are a standby in Christmas hospitality give cheer to the guest and reputation to the hostess.

Favourite home drinks today are:

HOT	COLD
cup of cocoa	coffee
cup of soup	summer cup
mulled home-made wine	barley water
cup or glass of coffee	home-made ginger wine

For soup, so restorative to the tired late worker, there are, in addition to the tinned soups (to which simple other ingredients can bring endless variety), many quickly prepared appetising soups. When the housewife has a little leisure she sometimes likes to prepare a more unusual soup such as the famous bortsch for her guests.

Ideas for cheery hot drinks are :—

Home-made wine, with hot water, powdered cinnamon, allspice or cloves to bring out flavour, and sugar or syrup to sweeten.

If the home cellar should run to it, try a small dessertspoonful of rum with a few drops of orange essence and a teaspoonful of sugar in tumbler filled up with boiling water. Add grated orange rind.

Cider, so popular in summer cups, is good mulled in winter. Still cider is used, putting it in saucepan over gentle heat with a little sugar, and some or all of the following spices to taste—cinnamon, ground ginger, cloves, nutmeg. A good Christmas festivity drink.

BLACKBERRY SYRUP

3 lbs. blackberries.   1 lb. golden syrup.

Cover blackberries with a little water and simmer until soft. Put in jelly bag to drip. Stir one pound of golden syrup or treacle in 2 pints of juice, and simmer again until syrupy consistency.

Dilute in hot water for drinks. To make sweets : add 3 dessertspoonfuls (¾ oz.) gelatine to half a pint of syrup and cut in lozenges when cold. Both excellent for sore throats.—L. D. FUGERE, The Lynches, Whitchurch, Oxfordshire.

COFFEE MAKING

Throughout the United States one is never offered coffee with hot or boiling milk. Coffee there means a full cup of good strong coffee served with a very small jug of cream or creamy milk, cold, just to "top" it.—A. N., York.

A good coffee can be made from 1 tablespoonful coffee (heaped for strong coffee) per person to 1 large cupful water.

All types of filters or infusers produce the same result in a variety of ways. The essentials are a perfect infusion with boiling water and a reliable fine strainer, according to the director of a firm of coffee importers. Good coffee can be made in a saucepan.

As good a way as any is to make beverages in a jug. Measure in the coffee, pour the correct amount of boiling water over, mix with spoon, allow to stand 3 to 5 minutes, strain off through a piece of muslin. Re-heat.

All forms of trick recipes concocted with the object of shrouding the making of coffee with an aura of mystery are condemned by this expert—pinches of pepper, salt, white of egg, and so on.

To sum up : Make sure that the blend is correct—a good coffee. Do not stint in measurement. Infuse in boiling water. Do not boil. Strain through fine strainer. Serve hot.

FRUIT CUP

½ pint stewed apple juice.
4 saccharine tablets.
3 teaspoonfuls lemonade powder or crystals.

Bunch of mint.
Cucumber peel.
Apple peel

Put all ingredients in 2-pint glass jug and stir until lemonade powder and saccharine is dissolved. Fill up jug with water and ice, if available, stir well and leave for 10 minutes before drinking in order to get full flavour of mint. A few leaves of borage and marjoram are a good addition.—MRS. D. COOMBS, 2K, Portman Mansions, W.1.

FRUIT SHAKE

Put milk into bowl and add fruit juice, fresh or from stewed fruit cooked with only enough water to prevent burning. Add a drop or two at a time, beating briskly. Allow 1-1½ oz. fruit juice to ½ pint milk. Ice-cream may be added—1 teaspoonful to ½ pint milk.—M. M., London, W.1.

LEMON SQUASH FOR STORE

5 small lemons.
1½ lbs. sugar.

1 pint boiling water.
½ oz. tartaric or citric acid.

Peel lemons thinly so that no pith is used. Put rind in large bowl, squeeze juice over. Cover with sugar. Pour over boiling water, stirring till sugar has dissolved, add tartaric or citric acid; stir well. Cover and leave 24 hours, stirring occasionally, strain. Bottle, cork tightly. A refreshing hot or cold drink, dilute to taste. Oranges can be used instead.—I. M. C., Kenton.

MINT JULEP

1 teacupful mint leaves.
½ teaspoonful orange essence.

1 pint boiling water.
Sugar to taste.
Few drops green colouring (optional)

Slightly crush mint leaves and put into stoneware jug. Pour boiling water over leaves and leave to infuse. When cold sweeten to taste and flavour with orange essence. A few drops of green colouring matter may be added. Pour into tall glasses, decorate with sprig of mint. This should be served icy cold to be at its best.

MULLED ALE

1 pint bitter beer.	2 reconstituted eggs.
½ pint old ale.	⅛ teaspoonful grated nut-
1 tablespoonful sugar	meg or mixed spice.

Well beat the eggs and put with sugar and spice into warm bowl. Put beer and ale into saucepan and bring almost to boiling point. Pour hot liquid over egg mixture. Whisk all ingredients and keep as hot as possible.—*The Daily Telegraph* HOME COOK.

*   *   *   *   *

SOUPS FOR TO-DAY

BORTSCH

The beetroot soup of Russia must always be soured.
Quantities for 6–8 persons :

2 large raw beetroots.	Parsley.
9 cupfuls stock or water.	Bayleaf.
2 ozs. margarine.	Salt and pepper.
1 onion.	2 tablespoonfuls vinegar.
2 carrots.	⅛ cupful of flour.
2 or 3 sticks of celery	

Cut all vegetables except beetroot in thin strips and simmer two hours in skimmed stock previously brought to the boil. Beetroot and vinegar are treated separately. Wash and clean beetroot and cut in strips. Melt margarine in a pan, put in strips of beetroot and moisten with vinegar. Heat, stirring all the time, adding flour.

Still stirring, moisten from time to time with spoonfuls of stock till beetroot is almost cooked. Add beetroot mixture to stock and simmer till cooked. Beetroot must not be overcooked, as colour is destroyed.—W. C. B., London, N.12.

LAST MINUTE SOUP

Dissolve meat cube or essence in quantity of water required and add distinctive flavouring such as celery salt or seed, grated carrot, onion juice, dash of cayenne, pinch of ground mace or a little vinegar from the pickled walnut jar. Tomato juice or cooked puree are other finishes.—THE HOME COOK.

PEA POD SOUP AND DUMPLINGS

1 lb. pea pods.	1 teaspoonful sugar.
4 ozs. peas.	2 tablespoonfuls milk.
1 onion.	Knob of margarine.
Sprigs of mint.	Pepper, salt.
½ oz. flour.	

Wash pods and put into saucepan with sliced onion and mint, and just enough cold water to cover. Bring to boil. Simmer gently till tender. Drain and either rub pods through sieve or scrape off the soft lining to the pods. Reheat liquid they were boiled in, add pea puree, sugar, flour blended with the cold milk, salt and pepper and margarine. Bring to boil; if too thick add a little milk. Serve with dumplings.

Dumplings

2 ozs. flour.	1 tablespoonful chopped
1 oz. fat.	parsley.
1 reconstituted egg.	Salt, pepper.
Pinch of nutmeg.	

Mix all dry ingredients together. Mix to soft dough with egg. Drop teaspoonfuls into boiling soup and simmer 5 minutes.

POTATO ROSE VELOUTÉ

This soup is an attractive colour and the oatmeal makes it deliciously smooth. Quantities enough for four people.

¼ lb. potatoes.	2 tablespoonfuls chopped
1 quart water.	celery stems or leaves.
1 tablespoonful fine oatmeal.	1 slice of raw beetroot.
	Salt, pepper.
2 tablespoonfuls chopped onion or leeks.	Bayleaf.
	Nutmeg to taste.
2 shredded sprouts.	

Put water in pan. Slice in all vegetables finely to save cooking time. Boil up, sift in oatmeal, boil up again. Add salt and pepper, bayleaf, nutmeg. Strain.

Six minutes before serving add beetroot, cook till soup is nicely coloured. Take out beet. Serve hot with raw shredded sprouts sprinkled in each plate.—L. FRANCES, 6 Boscobel Road, St. Leonards-on-Sea.

PUMPKIN SOUP

2 lbs. pumpkin.	1 reconstituted egg.
1 onion.	Water to cover.
1 oz. margarine.	Milk as required.
Salt and pepper to taste.	

Peel pumpkin, remove seeds, slice. Put in pan with chopped onion and water to cover. When cooked, sieve, add salt, pepper and margarine. Return to heat, dilute with milk or milk and water—soup is of the thick creamy kind. Bring to boil. Just before serving, when soup has stopped boiling, add well-beaten egg and serve.—*The Daily Telegraph* HOME COOK.

D

TOMATO SOUP

1 lb. tomatoes.
A few bacon rinds.
1 onion.
1 stick of celery or pinch of celery salt.
¼ teaspoonful sugar.

1 oz. flour.
1 oz. dripping.
1 pint stock or water.
1 gill household milk.
Pepper, salt.

Melt dripping in saucepan, fry bacon rinds, sliced onion, tomatoes and celery. Cook 15 minutes without browning with lid on. Add stock or water. Simmer gently 30 minutes. Sieve and return to pan. Bring to boil. Mix flour with a little cold milk, add to soup, boil till it thickens and add rest of milk and sugar. Reheat.

WATERCRESS SOUP

4 ozs. watercress.
1½ pints vegetable stock.
¼ pint milk or milk and water.
½ lb. potatoes.

1 chopped leek or sliced onion.
Seasoning.
1 reconstituted egg
1 oz. margarine.

Add grated raw potatoes and leek to stock in saucepan. When soft, mash in pan with wooden spoon. Season. Chop watercress, cook gently in saucepan with margarine. Add to it potato and liquid, also milk. Just before serving, add well beaten egg.

Chapter IV. STORE SNACK SHELF

CHEESE SPREAD

½ lb. grated cheese.
1 oz. margarine.
2 tablespoonfuls fresh milk.
2 teaspoonfuls vinegar.
1 teaspoonful pepper.

2 teaspoonfuls Worcester sauce (or other relish).
2 teaspoonfuls made mustard.
1 saltspoonful salt.

Melt margarine, add milk, grated cheese and other ingredients. Simmer slowly until thick and creamy and cheese is quite melted, stirring gently all the time. Pour into small jars, cover with greaseproof paper and lids if available. This spread will keep 6 weeks to 2 months.—L., Church, Crookam.

CHOCOLATE BUTTER

4 heaped teaspoonfuls cocoa.	2 ozs. margarine.
	4 dessertspoonfuls sugar.
2 teaspoonfuls cornflour.	1 teacupful milk.

Mix cocoa and cornflour into a paste with about half the milk. Boil the remaining milk. Stir milk into paste and boil for 4 minutes. Remove saucepan from heat and place in bowl of cold water. Cream margarine and sugar, then gradually stir in cooled mixture, beating all the time with a fork. Put in jars and tie down. This makes about ½ lb. and keeps well.—ANNE WILLIAMS, Holly Bank, Banwell, Somerset.

LEMON CURD

(1)

2 ozs. margarine.	2 dried eggs (reconstituted).
Lemon juice substitute (equal to juice of 1 lemon).	4 ozs. sugar.
	Few drops lemon essence.

Stir ingredients over gentle heat in double pan till mixture thickens.

If crystals are preferred to other lemon substitutes, omit the two flavourings mentioned above and add instead to mixture in pan 3 heaped teaspoonfuls lemonade crystals dissolved in 3 tablespoonfuls water. Quantity of crystals can be varied to suit taste.

A basin placed over saucepan of boiling water may take place of double saucepan, or ingredients can be mixed in jam-jar and cooked in this in saucepan of water. Jar is then ready to be tied down when curd is cooked. Quantities given make 1 lb.—K. B., Shoreham.

(2)

1 lb. sugar.	6 ozs. margarine.
5 dried eggs, reconstituted (using 8 and not the usual 10 tablespoonfuls water).	1 teaspoonful citric acid dissolved in 4 tablespoonfuls water.
	Lemon essence to taste.

Melt margarine in double saucepan, add sugar, citric acid dissolved in water, and beaten reconstituted eggs. Stir constantly until mixture thickens. Add lemon essence until lemon flavour can be tasted. Put into pots.—MRS. N. M. HOGG, 49 King's End, Ruislip, Middlesex.

MINCEMEAT

2 lb. apple pulp.	1 lb. chopped fruit.
6 ozs. sugar.	4 oz. candied peel.
4 ozs. margarine or suet.	¼ teaspoonful ratafia essence.
¼ teaspoonful grated nutmeg.	¼ teaspoonful powdered orange rind.

Mix together over moderate heat till ingredients are well merged—about 20 minutes. Essence not to be added till removal from heat. Not intended for long keeping. One dessertspoonful rum will improve mincemeat.—*The Daily Telegraph* HOME COOK.

MOCK FOIE GRAS

4 ozs. cooked liver (ox liver will do if well cooked, or liver sausage)	1½ ozs. margarine or beef dripping.
2 rashers fat bacon.	Few sliced dates or raisins.
1 dessertspoonful grated onion.	Sprinkling of cayenne.
	Dry mustard, salt.

Mince liver and bacon twice. Cook onion in fat, add minced mixture and sliced fruit, sprinkling with seasoning. Bring gently to boiling point and pot.—ANN GORE DAVIDS, 27 Upper Montagu Street, W.1.

WINTER BREAKFAST SPREAD

A good way to use up surplus fats is to render down and clarify in usual manner, mixing different varieties. Take a meat cube, crush into powder with a fork, and just as the fat, which has been poured into a bowl, is beginning to set, stir in crushed cube and beat well in. When cold this makes tasty and appetising breakfast spread, saving butter or margarine.—A. L. C., Dartford.

SECTION IV
STOCKING THE STORE CUPBOARD

Chapter I. FRUIT BOTTLING and VEGETABLE PRESERVING

FRUIT bottling has once again become an important part of housecraft and thousands of novices in recent seasons have successfully attempted the important task of preserving fruit surplus for winter use by this means.

Methods are nowadays given wide publicity, ranging from the advertising columns of the Press from which the Food Ministry gives guidance to the housewife during each bottling season to excellent leaflets issued by industrial organisations dealing with this important aspect of the nation's food stores.

This chapter therefore is devoted in the main to the special treatment required by various fruits and vegetables which it is desired to preserve either by bottling, drying or in salt.

One word of warning to amateurs in this highly technical field. Whatever the method of bottling chosen, directions must be followed precisely. All-important is realisation of the fact that it is useless to hope for the best.

FRUIT STERILISATION WITHOUT OVEN OR PAN

This method saves trouble and can be very satisfactory. Try first with a small quantity of fruit. The following recipe comes from a reader and has been used in a busy farmhouse kitchen for years.

(1) Scald jars, rubber rings and glass tops in boiling water, brush inside metal screw tops with a little melted fat to obviate rust in storage.

(2) Dry jars, stand on board or wooden table. Whilst hot, pack closely with fruit, pressing gently with wooden spoon if necessary.

(3) Place warm cloth round jar and pour boiling water over fruit, covering completely. Pour this off immediately.

(4) Cover fruit again with boiling water, but this time to within one inch of top of jar.

(5) Fix on rubber ring, put on glass top, screw on metal top as tightly as possible.

(6) When jars are quite cold, unscrew metal cap and test. If glass top does not come away, the seal is complete and metal cap can be screwed on tightly again.

(7) If glass top does come away pour off water and repeat process. Should jar again not be sealed, use up fruit and examine jar, rubber ring and glass top for cause of leakage.—MRS. S. M. DELANEAUX COOKE, Coney Grey, The Slough, Redditch.

SACCHARINE

This sweetening agent cannot be used for bottling. It makes some fruit bitter.

PEARS (To Bottle)

Choose large, firm pears, not too ripe. Peel, cut in half lengthways, remove cores. Plunge immediately into pan of boiling water, boil 5–10 minutes until soft but still firm and unbroken. This keeps pears a good colour.

Lift out, pack in warm jars. Fill jars up with boiling water in which pears were done, and seal.

If it is desired to do them in syrup—a big improvement—when pears are lifted out of boiling water, lay them carefully on one side while sugar is added to water ($\frac{1}{4}$ lb. sugar to 1 pint water is sufficient), allow to dissolve and boil up a few minutes till clear. Pack pears in warm jars, as before, fill up with boiling syrup and seal.—S. E., Macclesfield.

Second Method

6 lb. almost ripe pears	$1\frac{1}{2}$ lbs. sugar.
(William if possible).	1 quart water.
$\frac{1}{4}$ pint best white vinegar.	

Peel, cut pears in halves and core. As you do this, drop them into cold water to preserve colour. Make a syrup of vinegar, sugar and water, put pears in, boil $\frac{1}{2}$ hour or until tender. Put into jars and pour syrup over, fasten down hot.—N. G., Bletchley.

RASPBERRIES (To Retain Colour When Bottled)

Raspberries deteriorate rapidly. Preserve immediately after picking. If possible pick straight into jars to save handling as they bruise easily. Remove stalks carefully.

Fill up bottles with sound dry raspberries, place near bottom of oven in moderate heat—if gas set at Mark 3. Place lids on bottles, let them cook gently till steam begins to rise. Meanwhile put some raspberries in a saucepan with water barely covering the fruit and let them boil. Now take out bottles, one at a time, lift lid and fill up with boiling juice, quickly put on rubber ring and cover and clip or screw down immediately.

When cold, the lids should be on so firmly that screw tops or clips cannot be removed.—G. F., Crowborough.

RHUBARB TO BOTTLE

In recent seasons rhubarb has been bottled for the first time in many homes.

Cut up rhubarb, place in bottling jars, cover with water to which a few drops of pink colouring have been added. No sugar needed. Place jars in preserving pan three parts filled with cold water and bring slowly to boil, then immediately remove from heat so that rhubarb does not go to pieces. Remove jars after a few moments and screw tightly.—K. F. D., Salisbury.

Rhubarb can be preserved uncooked with tablets.

*   *   *   *   *

TOMATOES

(a) BOTTLING

Method of bottling tomatoes, whether in their own juice or in water depends on their use, whether required whole or not. Tomatoes bottled in their juice break and become more of a puree, but flavour is better.

Tomatoes need more sterilising than most fruit; housewives often under-sterilise and tomatoes go mouldy. Sterilising times given below should be strictly observed.

Jars will need to be filled up from an extra jar of fruit after sterilis-ing; particularly in case of tomatoes cooked in their own juice.

*   *   *   *   *

Remove stalks from small tomatoes, not too ripe. Pack tightly into hot jars, tapping each jar on folded cloth to shake fruit down. Do not break skins.

Sterilised in own juice:

After packing in bottles sprinkle tomatoes with salt (1 teaspoonful to 1 lb. tomatoes), put on lids, sterilise in oven (1½ hours at 240 degs. or mark 1), or in water, taking 1½ hours to bring water to 190 degs. (i.e. simmering point). Keep simmering 30 minutes, do not let it gallop. Water should come to top of jars. Remove a jar at a time from heat, tighten screw tops and next day test seal.

Bottled in water:

Add ½ oz. salt for each quart of boiling water with which fruit is covered. Sterilise either by oven or water method.

(b) PULP OR PUREE

Cut ripe tomatoes into quarters. Allow 1 teaspoonful each of sugar and salt to every 2 lb. tomatoes. Simmer till tender, using only enough water to prevent burning, 30 minutes approximately. Stir frequently.

Press through coarse sieve and pour at once into warmed jars. Seal with rings and lids as for bottled fruit. Place jars in saucepan of hot water, standing them on slabs of wood or wire rack. Water should come up to top of jars. Bring to boil, boil 15 minutes. Remove jars, tighten screw tops, store in cool place.—MRS. P. Kyle, Kildare, Burwash, Sussex.

This is one of the most all-round additions to store, for it can be used in making soups, stews, entrees, fillings and sauces.

APPLE SLICES FROM WINDFALLS

Peel windfall apples, cut out bad parts and cores. Slice fairly thinly. Drop into solution of 2 oz. salt to 1 gallon of water. Remove after 5 minutes. Place slices on wire trays. Dry gradually either in sun, cool oven, warming rack or hot airing cupboard, taking several days if necessary. Ready when like chamois leather. Will keep indefinitely.—E. M. G., Mortimer West.

APPLE RINGS

These are prepared in the same way as the slices, cut into ¼ inch thick rings, and dipped as before into salt solution. Thread on sticks or arrange on wire trays. Place in very cool oven or dry in warm room or airing cupboard. Drying may take some days; rings are ready when texture resembles chamois leather. Leave 12 hours before storing in dry place.

CANDIED ORANGE CIRCLES

Soak half circles of orange peel in slightly salted water 3 days. Drain, boil in clean water till soft, drain again. Make syrup by boiling two cupfuls sugar and one cupful water 5 minutes. Place orange peel in basin, pour syrup over, leave 6 days. Strain off syrup into saucepan, bring to boil. Put in orange rinds and boil 15 minutes.

Lift peel on to dish carefully, pour syrup over, filling up each half with syrup. Sprinkle over with sugar, dry in cool oven.—E. H., Streatham.

CUCUMBERS FOR WINTER USE

Outdoor or frame cucumbers may be preserved by this method, similar to that for beans.

Pare and slice cucumber. Place layer of salt in small wide-mouthed jar (1 lb. jars are suitable). Place 4 or 5 slices flat in jar, cover with half-inch layer of salt to each inch of cucumber, pressing down lightly. Proceed with alternate layers, finishing with one of salt. Tie down with dry paper and elastic band. In two days contents will have shrunk and jars must be filled up by the same process till no more shrinkage occurs, when jars should be finally sealed down with screw tops or transparent covers.

To use, soak in cold water for 6 hours, changing it once or twice. Serve either plain or in vinegar.—L. B. P., Hayling Island.

Another method

Wipe cucumber with damp and then dry cloth. Seal cut end of stalk with sealing wax or paint over with white of egg. Cucumbers are then hung like marrows and keep till Christmas.

ORANGE POWDER

Remove skin of fruit, taking away white pith. Bake skin in oven until thoroughly dry. When dry and brittle, pound or put through fine mincer until reduced to powder. Store in wide-necked bottle tightly corked. ½-teaspoonful in cake or pudding will give the true fruit flavour.—A. D. GRAVES, Claremont, Northwood.

QUICK ORANGE PEEL

Peel of 3 oranges.	A little granulated sugar.
1 teacupful loaf sugar.	Water.

Cut peel in sections, put in pan and cover with water, boil till white pith can be scraped off with spoon. Drain peel. Put loaf sugar and 1 tablespoonful water into saucepan; when sugar has dissolved add peel cut in strips, cook gently till it is transparent, when it will have absorbed nearly all syrup. Lift with fork, roll in granulated sugar. Leave on wire tray till cool and dry. Store in airtight glass jar.— A. E. J., Old Hunstanton.

RUNNER BEANS—SALTING

Salting of beans, runner and French, makes a valuable contribution to the winter store.

Three essentials for success are very young beans straight off plant if possible, plenty of salt and tight packing. Do not wash beans; they must be quite dry when put into jar. Place thick layer of salt at bottom of 7 lb. stone jar and gradually fill with alternate layers of thinly sliced beans (they pack better so but if small may be left whole) and salt, pressing salt firmly down each time, especially at the sides. Top layer must be of salt. Tie down and after three days open. Contents will have dropped about two inches. Press down firmly again and continue with layers. Repeat process for a third time after another three days, putting thick layer of salt on top. Cover with several layers of paper firmly tied down.—D. M. W., Midhurst.

To cook Beans

Take out quantity required. Push remainder under brine and cover again securely. Put beans in colander, wash out salt under tap. Cover with cold water, just bring to boil, strain this water off and have ready enough boiling water to cover beans. Cook till tender.—E. F. C. Crowborough.

Reasons for failure

(1) Insufficient salt. (2) Using table instead of brick salt. (3) Using stale or damp beans. (4) Neck of vessel not large enough.

How much salt ? Official Ministry of Food advice is 1 lb. to every 3 lbs. beans but many housewives use more.

Jars may vary from 2 lb. glass jar to large earthenware crock. Suitable covering is a close fitting lid or several layers of brown paper tied with string.

TO PRESERVE NUTS

Hazel nuts can be gathered as soon as they drop off the stalk at a touch. If picked before they will not keep. They and any other kind of nut may be treated by the following recipe.

Shell nuts, dry in very slow oven or on thin tin placed over the cool oven of a kitchen range. Leave till dried through. Then place in airtight tins and use as required in cakes and puddings.

(1) Ground on an ordinary nutmeg grater they are delicious in cakes or Christmas puddings in place of almonds.

(2) Chopped for the outside decoration of fruit cakes. Sprinkled over jam filling of sponge sandwich.

(3) Used for "butter" filling (margarine and milk beaten to a cream to which a good handful of chopped nuts is added) for sponge sandwich —E. A. H., Basingstoke.

Other methods

(a) Hazel nuts are delicious if baked in their shells in rather a slow oven till light brown. Shell them and you have a crisp kernel.— M. P., Pembury.

(b) Bury nuts in the ground (sprinkling them first if liked with a little salt) packing them in airtight tins or in boxes. They do not shrivel this way as they do when dried.

Chapter II CHUTNEYS, PICKLES, SALAD CREAMS AND BOTTLED SAUCES

BEETROOT PICKLE

THIS is an excellent accompaniment to cold meat.

3 lbs. beetroots.
¼ lb. sugar.
2 large onions.
1¼ lbs. cooking apples.

2 teaspoonfuls ground ginger.
1 pint vinegar.
1 dessertspoonful salt.

Boil beet in usual way till soft. Peel beetroot, put with onions and apples through mincer, boil in vinegar with other ingredients till onions and apples are cooked.—E. M. T., Littlehampton.

GOOSEBERRY AND RHUBARB CHUTNEY

1¼ lbs. gooseberries and ¼ lb. rhubarb *or* 2 lbs. green tomatoes.
4 small onions.
¾ pint vinegar.
1 small teaspoonful pepper.

1¼ teaspoonfuls salt.
1¼ teaspoonfuls mixed mustard.
2½ tablespoonfuls golden syrup *or* 6 ozs. demerara sugar.

Top and tail, wash and dry gooseberries. Cut up rhubarb in 2 inch pieces. (If green tomatoes are used instead of gooseberries and rhubarb, fry them first.) Chop onions. Put in pan with other ingredients. Cook gently until a good consistency, stirring frequently. Leave to cool, pot and cover.

GOOSEBERRY SYRUP CHUTNEY

Fill a big stone jar with a layer of whatever is in season—green gooseberries or green tomatoes and so on. Next a layer of chopped onion and a third layer of sultanas or dates. The three layers together should be about 3 inches deep. Pour over one tablespoonful syrup, sprinkle with very little salt. Repeat layers till jar is almost full, pour in vinegar to cover.

Bake slowly in oven until a rich brown.

GREEN MINT SAUCE FOR STORE

¼ lb. chopped mint.
¾ pint vinegar.

½ lb. sugar.

Boil vinegar and pour it over the sugar. Stir till dissolved, then add chopped mint. Bottle when cold. When required, sauce can be diluted with a little water. The mint retains its greenness.—E. M. G., Harrow Weald.

GREEN TOMATO CHUTNEY

10 lbs. tomatoes.
2 quarts vinegar.
2 lbs. sugar.
1 sliced onion.
Salt.

¼ lb. in all of cloves, ground cinnamon, peppercorns.
Pinch of cayenne.

Slice tomatoes, sprinkle each layer with salt; let them remain till next day. Then drain salt away, put tomatoes into preserving pan with vinegar, sugar, sliced onion and spices. Simmer gently till tender; store in medium size bottles, cork and seal.—Mrs. A. S. Jessup, 80 Cross-lane East, Gravesend.

GREEN TOMATO SWEET PICKLE

2 lbs. chopped green tomatoes.
¾ lb. peeled, cored and sliced apples.
¼ lb. chopped onions.
Saltspoonful cayenne pepper.

½ pint vinegar.
4 ozs. sultanas, raisins or chopped prunes.
¾ lb. sugar.
1 small teaspoonful ground ginger.

Boil all ingredients together till thick and stiff like jam. Pour into small pots. Seal and keep in cool, dry place.—Mrs. Hume-Spry, Twynax, Farnham, Surrey.

HORSERADISH SAUCE

This keeps a year. Shred horseradish, pack it in screw top bottle or jar. Boil sufficient vinegar for two minutes; when it is cold pour over horseradish to cover. Screw on top of jar.

When sauce is required, blend small quantity with pepper, salt, pinch of mustard, sufficient cream (top of milk or unsweetened tinned milk) and vinegar.—M. M. G., Tenterden.

MINT JELLY (No vinegar required)

6 to 8 ozs. fresh mint.
2 lbs. unripe gooseberries or sour green apples.
1 quart water.

Sugar.
1 lemon or lemon substitute or 1 teaspoonful of citric acid.
Green colouring.

Wash fruit (if apples, cut up, do not peel or core). Put fruit, water lemon and bunch of mint into preserving pan. Cook till fruit is well pulped. Strain through jelly bag, allowing to drip undisturbed.

Measure liquid, boil up and add ¾ lb. sugar to 1 pint. Dissolve sugar, boil again and test for setting. Add green colouring at first signs of setting, also a little chopped mint if liked. Pot and cover. A good substitute for redcurrant jelly.

MIXED FRUIT CHUTNEY

6 lbs. fruit.	¼ lb. raisins (optional).
1 lb. onions.	1 large teaspoonful salt.
1 lb. sugar.	Spiced vinegar.

Use any fruit, apples, pears, damsons, plums, green tomatoes or, earlier in the year, gooseberries. Fruit that is not too ripe is best. Wash, peel, core, stone according to what is necessary and cut up or put through coarse mincer.

Put fruit and chopped onions in pan, cover with spiced vinegar and boil till cooked. Add sugar, raisins if desired and salt. Stir well till sugar is dissolved, bottle, and when cold cover with greaseproof paper.—MRS. G. CURTIS, 253 Avondale Avenue, Esher, Surrey.

Spiced Vinegar

1 quart vinegar.	2 tablespoonfuls chopped
¼ oz. allspice.	onion.
¼ oz. cloves.	2 oz. grated horseradish.
2 oz. peppercorns.	2 bay leaves.
1 oz. ground ginger.	¼ oz. salt.
2 cloves garlic.	

Put all ingredients into pan and simmer 15 minutes. Strain.

MOCK CAPERS

Gather nasturtium seeds on a dry day. Wipe them, pack into dry bottles; these should be three parts full. Fill up with vinegar which has been brought to the boil with salt and peppercorns added in the proportion of 1 dessertspoonful salt and 6 peppercorns to each pint.

Cork the bottles tightly while still hot and leave two months before using

PICKLED WALNUTS

Pickle walnuts while still young and green before any tendency to woodiness has set in. Prick walnuts with fork or large darning needle, put in earthenware crock, cover with brine. This is made of 6 oz. block salt dissolved in 1 quart hot water, and used when cold. Keep walnuts covered with wooden tray or plate for a week, turning over each day. Change brine after this, leave another six days. Drain, spread out on a dish in the sun; they will turn black in a day. Leave until they do so. Put into wide-mouthed glass jars and cover with spiced vinegar.

To make Spiced Vinegar

1 quart vinegar.	1 oz. whole ginger,
1 oz. black peppercorns.	bruised.
1 oz. mustard seed.	½ teaspoonful salt.
4 cloves.	1 or 2 cloves garlic.
2 blades mace.	

Boil all together 10 minutes. Cool, repeat boiling; when cold pour over walnuts in jars, distributing spices; cover jars. Pickle must be kept covered with vinegar. Fill up with ordinary vinegar from time to time.—*The Daily Telegraph* HOME COOK.

PLUM SAUCE

To every pound of plums allow:

¼ pint vinegar.	6 crushed peppercorns.
6 ozs. sugar.	1 chilli pod.
1 teaspoonful salt.	½ teaspoonful mixed
2 small onions.	spice.
3 cloves.	

Put all into pan with a lid. Bring to boil slowly, then simmer half an hour. Leave till cold. Take out onions, sieve the sauce. Boil 5 minutes, bottle.—MRS. C. WELLWOOD, School, Llangynidr, Crickhowell, Brecon.

RED CABBAGE PICKLE

1 red cabbage.	2 pints spiced vinegar.
Salt.	

Remove outer leaves of cabbage and hard stalk from centre. Shred cabbage finely, pile on a large dish, sprinkling each layer of cabbage with a good handful of salt. Place a dish on top and let it stand 48 hours. Strain off liquid, shake cabbage dry.

Pack into jars and pour over cold spiced vinegar made as for mixed fruit chutney. Vinegar must cover cabbage. Tie down firmly.

SALAD CREAM FOR STORE

(1)

1 reconstituted egg.	½ oz. margarine.
1 level tablespoonful	1 cupful vinegar.
flour.	1 teaspoonful mustard.
1 heaped tablespoonful	Pinch of salt.
sugar.	Sprig of thyme.

Mix vinegar, fat and sugar in saucepan and bring nearly to boil (care must be taken not to let it boil). Mix remaining ingredients separately, except thyme. Pour hot mixture over slowly, stirring all the time. Put in saucepan and cook all for 5 minutes, stirring. Thyme is put in just before the end and removed later. Bottle in hot jars while still warm. This cream keeps well and is diluted as required with vinegar or milk.—MRS. F. MORETON, 20 Findon Avenue, Telscombe, Sussex.

(2)

1 large tin unsweetened liquid milk.	1 gill vinegar.
3 dried eggs, reconstituted, or 2 fresh ones.	1 oz. mustard.
	Salt and pepper to taste.
¼ lb. sugar.	Knob of margarine.

Make up tin of milk to one pint with fresh or household milk. Beat eggs well. Put all into a pan and stir till contents thicken. A small piece of butter or margarine may be added at this stage.—MISS L. CANDLISH, The Monastery, Jervaulx, Near Ripon, Yorks.

SOUR-SWEET BLACKBERRY AND DAMSON RELISH

1½ lbs. ripe blackberries.	1 teaspoonful ground ginger.
1 lb. ripe damsons.	
½ pint vinegar.	1 teaspoonful ground mace.
3 tablespoonfuls black treacle or golden syrup or 6 ozs. sugar.	1 teaspoonful black pepper.
2 teaspoonfuls onion juice.	2 small dessertspoonfuls salt.

Put blackberries in pan with damsons and vinegar. Simmer till tender, remove damson stones, stir in ginger, mace, pepper, salt. Add treacle, syrup or sugar. Stir over low heat till thick, adding onion juice just before cooked. Pot and seal.—MRS. E. C. WALKER, 2 Goodwood Avenue, Hutton.

SPICED PEARS

4 lbs. hard pears.	3 cloves.
2 lbs. sugar.	½ pint vinegar.
1½ inch piece of cinnamon.	½ pint water

Peel, core and quarter pears. Boil all ingredients together till pears are rather soft. Put fruit in jars. Boil liquid till it thickens, cool and pour over pears. Pot, cover with paper, tie down with string.—A. URBACH, Southwood, Windermere.

TOMATO, APPLE AND DATE CHUTNEY
(Sugarless)

5 lbs. tomatoes.
1 lb. syrup and dates together.
3 lbs. apples.
1 lb. onions.

1½ pints spiced vinegar.
Salt and pepper.
A few chillies.
1 teaspoonful ground ginger

Slice tomatoes, apples and onions, place all ingredients in pan. Bring to boil, simmer slowly for about 3 hours on top of stove or in oven.

If sugar is available it can be used instead of dates or together with them to make up the pound. *Officially approved recipe.*

TOMATO SAUCE FOR STORE

4 lbs. tomatoes.
1 large onion.
½ oz. white pepper.
¼ oz. allspice.
Boiling water.
1 bay leaf.

1 oz. salt.
4 ozs. sugar (demerara if possible).
½ pint white vinegar.
¼ oz. cloves.

Put tomatoes into a bowl and pour boiling water over them. Stand a few minutes, then skin and cut into thick slices; cover with salt and stand 24 hours.

Put tomatoes into a preserving pan with sliced onion and cook until pulped. Pass the mixture through a coarse sieve or colander, working it through with a wooden spoon. Return to pan, add sugar, pepper and vinegar. Put spices in muslin bag, well crush, and add to mixture with bay leaf. Boil all together until sauce thickens. Remove spices and bottle sauce.—Mrs. PARSON, The Gables, Cippenham Lane, Slough, Bucks.

VEGETABLE MARROW PICKLE

2 lbs. peeled marrow.
1 lb. onions.
1 pint vinegar.
4 ozs. sugar.
3 chillies or cayenne.

½ oz. ground turmeric.
¼ oz. ground ginger.
¼ oz. mustard.
1 teaspoonful salt.

Boil vinegar, salt and spices together 10 minutes. Cut up marrow in small cubes, leave sprinkled with salt overnight. Next day drain and cook with spiced vinegar, chopped onion, and sugar till marrow is tender but not broken. Bottle.—*The Daily Telegraph* HOME COOK.

Chapter III.

JAMS, JELLIES and MARMALADES

APPLE JELLY

4 lbs. apples.
2 pints water.
Sugar (1 lb. to 1 pint of juice).

Lemon substitute, equivalent to ½ lemon.

Wash and cut up apples but do not peel or core. Put into preserving pan with the water. Bring to boil, simmer gently till fruit is soft and reduced to a pulp. Put into jelly bag or muslin and leave to drain all night; the juice should be of a thickish consistency.

Next day measure juice and bring to boil. Have sugar warming in the oven. Remove pan from heat, add sugar and lemon substitute, stir till sugar has dissolved. Put pan back over heat and bring to boil. Boil quickly till jelly sets when tested on cold plate.

BRAMBLE JELLY

Blackberries.
Sugar.

Water.

Gather blackberries that are not too ripe. Put them into a preserving pan and nearly cover with cold water. Bring to boil, simmer one hour.

Crush fruit with wooden spoon to extract juice. Strain through jelly bag, muslin or hair sieve. Leave to drain all night.

Next day measure juice. Allow ¾ lb. sugar to 1 pint of juice. Put sugar in the oven to warm. Boil juice 15 minutes, then add warmed sugar. Boil till it jellies; this point is reached when a little of the syrup sets quickly when tested on a cold plate.

CHERRY JAM

1 lb. cherries (weighed after stoning).

1 lb. sugar.
¼ cupful water.

Boil sugar and water together for 10 minutes, add fruit to syrup. Boil all together quickly till liquid jellies. Allow 35 to 40 minutes for this.

A good summer breakfast preserve. Put preferably in small jars.

DAMSON JAM

4 lbs. damsons.   A little water.
3 lbs. sugar.

Remove stalks from fruit, wash and dry damsons. Put them into preserving pan with very little water, heat slowly till juice begins to flow. Bring fruit to boil and boil rapidly a few minutes till soft. Remove from heat. Add the sugar, previously warmed in the oven. Stir till sugar has dissolved, then boil quickly till jam sets when tested on a plate. While cooking, remove as many stones as possible.

GREEN GOOSEBERRY JAM

4 lbs. green gooseberries   1½ pints water
4 lbs. sugar.

Top and tail gooseberries. Put into preserving pan with cold water, bring to boil. Simmer 15–20 minutes. Remove from heat, add sugar that has meanwhile been warming in the oven. Stir till sugar is dissolved, return to heat, boil rapidly for 5 minutes, then test for set. Once the sugar is in, too long boiling will spoil the colour.

GREEN TOMATO JAM

This delicate preserve requires less sugar than most jams. Many people advise using no flavouring as it takes away from the unusual flavour of the tomatoes. For those who like to add lemon or ginger, quantities are given ; with lemon essence the preserve resembles the taparee jam of India.

6 lbs. green tomatoes.   3 lbs. sugar.
1 teaspoonful lemon es-   ¼ teaspoonful salt.
   sence or 3 teaspoonfuls
   ground ginger.

Wash and cut up tomatoes into small pieces. Grease bottom of preserving pan or just cover with water to prevent burning. Put in tomatoes and salt, boil 1 hour. Add sugar, boil till it begins to stiffen, about an hour. Just before taking up, add essence.—D. B., Portishead.

HOME-MADE PECTIN

Half pint pectin added to 4 lbs. fruit will help to set preserves made from fruit with poor setting qualities.

Take 3 lbs. windfall apples, 1 pint water, simmer till tender, mash well, strain through jelly bag. Repeat the process with the pulp left in the muslin, add second quantity of juice to the first. The pectin is then ready for use.

LEMON MARMALADE

1   lb. lemons.   2½ pints water.
2¼ lbs. sugar.

Quantities make 5 lbs. Weigh saucepan. Put in water and whole lemons, simmer gently with lid on till tender (about 1 hour). Take out fruit, cut finely ; this is much easier when lemons have been cooked. Return to saucepan, weigh all together. Water and fruit should weigh 3 lbs. Add ¾ lb. sugar to each lb. fruit and liquid, allow sugar to dissolve over low heat. Bring to boil, boil 1 hour. Pot.—W. F. H., Bridport.

MARROW MARMALADE

2 lbs. vegetable marrow.   1 level dessertspoonful
2 lbs. Victoria plums.   ground ginger (op-
4 lbs. sugar.   tional).

Peel and stone the plums. Prepare marrow, and cut into small dice. Put plums and sugar into pan, heat till sugar melts, then add marrow. Keep at boiling point 15 minutes to draw juices, then boil fast one hour. If ginger is used, add it with the marrow.—MISS E. WILKIE, 201 Hamlet Gardens, Ravenscourt Park, W.6.

ORANGE RIND MARMALADE

Peel and pips from 1 lb.   1½ lbs. sugar.
  oranges.   1 dessertspoonful tinc-
1 lb. apples.   ture of quassia.
1 tablespoonful citric   Water.
  acid powder or lemon
  essence to taste

Cut up orange peel. Soak in 2 pints water for 24 hours. Cover pips with water.

Wash and cut up apples without removing peel or core and simmer in half a pint of water till soft. Put through sieve. Simmer orange peel till soft, about 1 hour. Add sieved apple, water from pips, sugar, quassia and flavouring. Quassia is optional ; it gives slightly bitter flavour.

Boil fast in large preserving pan about 30 minutes, stirring occasionally till it sets when tested on saucer. This makes 3½ to 4 lbs. of marmalade.—M. D. T., Marlow.

Another method

6 ozs. sweet orange rind.	3 pints water.
Sugar.	1 teaspoonful citric acid.

Boil orange rind in the water for 2 hours or till peel and juice measure from 1½ to 1¾ pints. Take out soft rind, put through mincer. Measure minced rind and liquid and to each pint add 14 ozs. sugar. Add citric acid. Boil all together for 40 to 50 minutes or (1) till marmalade turns slightly darker, (2) it makes thick bubbles, (3) it will set on a plate. Generally all three happen together.—N. S., Gloucester.

PLUM JAM

4 lbs. plums, any kind.	1 pint water.
3 lbs. sugar.	

Stone plums, crack stones with hammer and remove kernels.

Put fruit, water and kernels into preserving pan and simmer gently till fruit is tender. Add sugar, stir till dissolved. Bring to boil and boil rapidly 15–20 minutes. Test for setting.

RHUBARB MARMALADE

1 quart rhubarb	Lemon substitute or
1 lb. sugar.	ground ginger.

This makes a firm preserve. Wash and dry but do not peel rhubarb. Cut in cubes, measure in jug. To each quart add 1 lb. sugar, allow to stand overnight. Strain off syrup and boil it 20 minutes. Pour over rhubarb again.

Repeat on two more days this process of straining off syrup and boiling 20 minutes, then pouring over rhubarb, leaving it each time to stand overnight. Then boil rhubarb and syrup together for 20 minutes. At last boiling add lemon substitute to taste or ground ginger in the proportion of 1 teaspoonful to 1 lb. fruit.—M., Bournemouth.

SEEDLESS BLACKBERRY AND APPLE MARMALADE

4 lbs. blackbeerries.	1 lb. sugar to 1 lb. pulp.
2 lbs. sour apples.	1 pint water.

Peel, core and cut up apples. Pick over blackberries. Put all the fruit into preserving pan with the water. Cook until reduced to a pulp, stirring often to prevent burning. Rub through a sieve. Measure and put into preserving pan with sugar. Boil till it sets, about 20 minutes. Stir constantly. This is a good accompaniment to moulds or rice.

SEEDLESS SUMMER CONSERVE

4 lbs. raspberries.	Sugar.
2 lbs. red currants.	Water.

Prepare fruits, heat very slowly till quite soft—they must not simmer —about 45 minutes. Sieve. For every pint of juice and pulp take 1 lb. sugar. Make a syrup, allowing one coffee cupful water to each pound of sugar, dissolve sugar slowly, stirring all the time, and when melted bring to boil. As sugar stiffens to nougat, draw aside from heat and rapidly beat in juicy pulp, stirring vigorously. Do not heat again. Will set and keep well. These quantities make about 9½ lbs. conserve. —E. K. E., Harpenden.

SUGAR ECONOMY

Glucose or syrup are suitable as part substitutes for sugar in jam making provided that in either case the proportion used does not exceed 25 per cent of the usual quantity of sugar required.

One tablespoonful syrup weighs 2 ozs., 2 tablespoonfuls should be used to each ¾ lb. sugar.

Do not use syrup with fruits containing little pectin, as it has no setting qualities. These are raspberries, strawberries, cherries, plums and greengages, rhubarb, over-ripe fruit. Blackberries are rich in pectin while red and lack it when they reach the black stage.

SWEET SPICED APPLE PRESERVE

8 lbs. apples (weighed after being peeled and cored).	½ pint vinegar.
	¼ pint water.
6 lbs. sugar.	12 cloves.

Mix all together, leave standing overnight. Next morning place in saucepan with cloves tied in muslin bag. Bring to boil, cook 45 minutes, keeping well stirred to prevent burning. Pot and cover.

This is good in tarts and puddings of roly-poly type. A few currants or sultanas provide variety if desired. It keeps well till following year's apple crop comes along.—MRS. F. MILLS, 74 The Drive, Bexley, Kent.

VEGETABLE MARROW AND ELDERBERRY JAM

This is an excellent jam of out-of-the-ordinary flavour. Peel vegetable marrow, remove seeds, cut up in small pieces. Weigh, put into preserving pan with half the weight of stripped ripe elderberries. Boil together with a little water just to cover bottom of pan till soft.

Add sugar in proportion of ¾ lb. to each lb. of combined fruit and marrow. Boil till jam jellies. If liked flavouring such as ground ginger can be added just before the sugar, but jam is delicious without.— HON. ADELA DOUGLAS PENNANT, Windlesham, Wittingham, Sussex.

THE GINGERS

APPLE GINGER

Equal quantities of sugar and well-washed, peeled, cored and sliced apples.

½ pint water to each 2 lbs. fruit.
1 level teaspoonful ground ginger to each lb. of fruit.

Bring fruit and water to boil, boil 10 minutes. Simmer till fruit is well cooked, add sugar, stir frequently till melted. Bring to boil and boil 15 minutes. Simmer again till jam thickens and darkens. Stir frequently. Mix ginger in a little cold water and add.

As a variation one pound of marmalade mixed with 4 lbs. of the jam gives a delicious flavour.—Miss TONKS, Riverside Avenue, Holdenhurst, Bournemouth.

MARROW GINGER

2½ lbs. vegetable marrow (weighed after peeling and removal of seeds).
2 lbs. sugar.

1 oz. root ginger or ½ to ¾ oz. ground ginger (strength varies).
1 teaspoonful lemon juice or essence.

Put marrow, cut up into 1½ inch cubes, to stand overnight, with sugar and flavouring. Boil all together gently next day till syrup is thick and sets and pieces of marrow are transparent. No water required. Remove ginger if root kind is used. If ground ginger is substituted, taste during cooking before adding the extra ¼ oz. as if too much is used, the preserve may be uneatable.

RHUBARB AND FIG GINGER

3 lbs. rhubarb.
½ lb. figs.
3 teaspoonfuls ground ginger.

2¾ lbs. sugar.
Pinch of salt.
1 tablespoonful marmalade.

Cut up rhubarb and figs in small pieces, put in preserving pan with salt and ground ginger, put sugar over all. Allow to stand 24 hours. Bring to boil, let it boil about 30 minutes. Add marmalade while boiling.—M. R., Ashford.

This recipe can also be used, omitting figs and marmalade.

SECTION V

ART of FLAVOURING

By *The Daily Telegraph* HOME COOK

WARTIME flavourings that give attraction and even distinction to the ordinary foods described as "austerity fare" have brought all the skill and resource of good housewifery into practice in our home kitchens. This new understanding of the art of flavouring will make itself felt in post-war cookery. How to select, store and use the various herbs, spices and essences that bring out the qualities of fish, meat, fruit and vegetables is not only a highly important item in the culinary curriculum but it can be a fascinating hobby.

Women have become so keenly interested in this aspect of cookery that many of them choose to begin with the culture of the herbs. They are growing them in their gardens, where space is limited, in tubs and even in window boxes. Others have to rely on the greengrocer, buying them by the market bunch and drying and sifting in their own kitchens. Gas and electric cookers have made home drying a quick and easy process. Tastes are changing and many herbs little used at one time by cooks in general are being given a place in the store cupboards.

HERBS—
GROWING, DRYING, BLENDING

When home grown, choose a dry day for gathering. Just before they begin to flower is the proper moment. Tie up in small bunches; dry in the sun if that should be possible, but any oven after cooking is over is satisfactory. Herbs should be sufficiently dry to rub through sieve or between palms of hands. Strip leaves from stalks and take care to see that any sharp spikes are disposed of before putting in air-tight labelled bottles. The following list provides a guide to selection and use of herbs in the new cookery.

Parsley

Most popular of all herbs in its fresh state for all-the-year-round garnishing and much used, chopped finely, in giving flavour and colour to sauces, accompanying white fish, boiled mutton and as ingredient in made dishes. In fresh or dried form used in omelets.

Mint

Green, chopped finely, mixed with castor sugar and vinegar, makes the old favourite mint sauce with roast lamb, but demand for mint jelly for store is increasing. Sprigs of young mint decorate soft drinks, small leaves are chopped and used as sandwich fillings and to flavour cakes. Whole or chopped leaves go into green salads, sprigs are boiled with new potatoes and green peas. Powdered dried mint is last minute addition to pea soup.

MINT JELLY

1 cupful young mint leaves (chopped).	2 tablespoonfuls sugar.
½ pint vinegar (preferably white).	½ oz. gelatine (1 tablespoonful).
	1 gill hot water.

Gather mint, wash and dry on cloth. Strip leaves, chop finely and measure. Put in basin. Put vinegar in pan with sugar. Boil. Have ready gelatine dissolved in the hot water. Stir into vinegar. Pour on to chopped mint. Let it cool. Stir occasionally till on the point of setting. Fill small pots and seal.

A few drops of green vegetable colouring improve appearance. The more quickly the mint is chopped, the better the colour.

*   *   *   *   *

Mint flavoured jelly that can be served as accompaniment with hot or cold roast lamb or as a teatime preserve may be made by adding chopped leaves to apple jelly (see Jams) or by putting the whole leaves into jelly and straining before storing.

The Thymes

Lemon thyme finds much favour in present day cookery. Both varieties popular for flavouring vegetable main dishes, croquettes, meat stews, soups and forcemeats.

Marjoram

Imparts "home-made" flavour to sausages, pies, galantines and other dishes, hot and cold which figure in snack fare.

Sage

Much used with onions or onion flavourings in stuffings for pork, duck and Irish stew, and in herb puddings, shepherd's pie, rabbit.

Chervil

Always a favourite herb in French and Belgian cookery, now taking its place in English kitchens. Brings out flavour of carrots as in Carrots Vichy.

Tarragon

Fresh leaves of this aromatic plant give piquancy to salads; is wanted for many sauces particularly Tartare and in fish cookery generally. Most convenient way is to use in form of vinegar.

Tarragon Vinegar

Sprigs of tarragon. White vinegar. Put freshly gathered sprigs into wide-necked jars, cover with vinegar. Strain after a few days and bottle, corking well. Time allowed for infusion varies greatly. Some cooks allow only a day or two, others 2 or 3 weeks. A few drops give subtle flavour to fish spread. Mixed with grated cheese, margarine, made mustard, a while-you-wait spread is provided.

* * * * *

Chives

Now accepted substitute for onion flavouring. Cultivated by gardener cooks as border plant and also in window boxes. Freshly gathered the bright, grass-like leaves are chopped to go into salads. A flavouring in soups, stews and sauces. A potato, beetroot or cucumber salad can owe much to sprinkling of chopped chives. Wanted for Tartare sauce and herb-flavoured omelets.

Basil

Acquired taste but being used more freely now that cooks are experimenting in new ways. On the whole fresh leaves preferred. They go into salads and decorate cups and soft drinks

Savoury

Winter and summer. Flavours sausages, soups and stews Excellent in sauces and stuffings that go with pork and duck cookery'

* * * * *

Time can often be saved by preparing one or two dried herb mixtures.

MIXED HERB POWDER (Dried Herbs)

1 oz. thyme.	1 oz. parsley.
1 oz. lemon thyme	½ oz. chervil.
1 oz. marjoram.	

Rub into fine powder, mix well, and store in air-tight container. Addition of a powdered bay leaf optional. This makes good utility mixture for savoury dishes generally.

OMELET HERB MIXTURE (Dried Herbs)

2 oz. parsley.	½ oz. chervil.
1 oz. thyme.	½ oz. chopped chives
1 oz. marjoram.	(dried).

Proceed as before.

THE BOUQUET GARNI

The Bouquet Garni makes special appeal to gardener cooks able to gather a fragrant posy and tie it up in muslin for soup or stew. Sprigs of thyme, marjoram, parsley with addition of a bay leaf make up a simple bouquet.

*   *   *   *   *

THE FLOURISHING GREEN BAY TREE

THE green bay tree flourishes apace in new-time cookery. Modern housewives are learning to appreciate the value of the aromatic leaves that can impart such distinctive flavour to otherwise ordinary savoury and sweet dish. In meat and vegetable stews it gives something of the flavour of game; fish such as mackerel, herrings and sprats when served soused can owe much to a bay leaf. The bay leaf is good in tomato cookery, flavours galantines and other meat moulds attractively, and is helpful in sauces, both savoury and sweet.

Women who can gather the leaves from their own bay trees or who have friends with bountiful bay trees are fortunate, but it is a sign of the new days in cookery that the leaves, in whole and powdered form, are now included in the range of culinary herbs retailed in little packets.

Home cooks have scope for experiment in the wider use of bay leaves. It is desirable to find out what degree of the spicy flavour appeals to the family, for the direction "a bay leaf" is vague. Leaves vary in size, sometimes half, or even a quarter, of a leaf is sufficient.

*   *   *   *   *

HOW TO USE SPICES

FOR spices the housewife looks not to her own garden domain but to the East. A sprinkle of paprika over macaroni, spaghetti, vegetable marrow and cauliflower au gratin, haricot beans and potato croquettes appeals to the eye. The grating of nutmeg with French and runner beans, the dust of cinnamon over hot buttered toast, mixed spices as a variation from dried fruits in buns, and the use of a little, but not too much, mace in all manner of meat dishes are directions in which spices can vastly improve fare.

More ginger is being used in the new cookery which has turned to ground and root ginger to bring out fruit and vegetable flavours. Many comparatively modern preserves made from green tomatoes, marrows, pumpkins, blackberries, prunes and dates respond well to the addition of ginger. Cinnamon is a welcome finish to plain boiled cereals, including those served at breakfast. Often it suits new tastes better than the overworked grate of nutmeg. This last-named spice is excellent in stuffings.

So see to it that the home store is well equipped with ginger, nutmegs, mace (in blade and ground), cloves, vanilla pods, carraway or cummin seeds if liked, mixed spice, and, for savoury fare, allspice.

Mixed Spice

½ oz. ground black pepper, ½ oz. ground allspice, ¾ oz. ground ginger, 1 teaspoonful ground mace, ¼ oz. grated nutmeg, ½ teaspoonful powdered cloves.

* * * * *

ESSENCES

THESE form a flavouring group to themselves, and the variety in use has shown marked increase without any indication as yet that this interesting advance has reached its limit. To the little bottles of vanilla, almond, ratafia and lemon essences, orange, pineapple, banana, raspberry, strawberry, apricot and all manner of other fruity extracts have been added. Ginger, cloves and other spices have also taken their place in the concentrated bottled form. It is advisable to buy the best and, as a rule, in not too small quantity. Two oz. bottles are practical in the case of the essences in general use.

INDEX

www.panmacmillan.com

www.ingramcontent.com/pod-product-compliance
Ingram Content Group UK Ltd.
Pitfield, Milton Keynes, MK11 3LW, UK
UKHW040639280225
455688UK00002B/18